Jenny Thomas and Diane White

Australia • Brazil • Japan • Korea • Mexico • Singapore • Spain • United Kingdom • United States

Achievement English @ Year 12
2nd Edition
Jenny Thomas
Diane White

Text designer: Book Design Ltd
Cover designer: Book Design Ltd
Production controller: Siew Han Ong
Reprint: Jess Lovell

Any URLs contained in this publication were checked for currency during the production process. Note, however, that the publisher cannot vouch for the ongoing currency of URLs.

Acknowledgements
Our grateful thanks to all past and present colleagues who have so generously shared their expertise, creativity and resources. English departments thrive on your collegiality.
The authors and publisher wish to thank the following people and organisations for permission to use the resources in this textbook. Every effort has been made to trace and acknowledge all copyright owners of material used in this book. In most cases this was successful and copyright is acknowledged as requested. However, if any infringement has occurred the publishers tender their apologies and invite the copyright holders to contact them.

page 7, Faber and Faber Ltd for *The Jaguar*, Ted Hughes; page 8 and 92, RNZFB, Bayleys and Consortium for advertisement; page 12, Faber and Faber Ltd for *Roman Wall Blues*, W.H. Auden; page 14, HarperCollins Publishers for the extract from *The Shipping News*, Annie Proulx; page17, Maurice Gee for the extract from *The Widow*; page 20, Air New Zealand Panorama for Che's Way; page 28, Simon and Schuster for The Wasteland by Alan Paton; page 37, HarperCollins Publishers Ltd for the extract from *The Two Towers*, J.R.R. Tolkien; page 40, David Hill for 'Language police constantly looking to have the last word'; page 44, C.K. Stead for Correct language deserves more than just lip service; page 46, INCLEAN magazine (www.incleanmag.com.au) for Cleaning Green by Brian Young; page 48, Shonagh Koea for the extract from Madeline first published in *The Littledene Club Final* ed Gordon Mclauchlan, Tandem Press, 1992; page 52, Tribune Media Services Inc for Scary Kids, Dave Barry; page 58, Auckland University Press for the extract from *The Godwits Fly*, Robin Hyde; page 62, Independent for I know, let's sell weapons to a lunatic by Mark Steel; page 72, James K. Baxter Foundation for Farmhand, James K. Baxter, published in Collected Poems by James K. Baxter, Oxford University Press, Australia and New Zealand, 1988; page 47, Faber and Faber Ltd for Wind, Ted Hughes; page 56 and 106, Hone Tuwhare Estate for *Friend and Mad*; page 78, Oberon Press for *The Diver*, Robert Currie, from *Diving Into Fire*; page 80, Marty Smith for *Hat*; page 82, Bill Manhire for A Winter Christmas; page 84, Pearson Education Australia for The Sadness of Madonnas by Bruce Dawe; page 94, Burger King for advertisement; page 96, S.A.F.E. for advertisement; page 98, Kiwi Blue Natural Spring Water for label; page 100, Codorniu for advertisement; page 102, McCoy Fruit Juice for advertisement; page 106, Scott Smith for his Jamaican Rum advertisement; page 116, Andrew White for speech; page 126, New Zealand Herald for There's much to learn from Tiger Mothers by Tapu Misa; page 131, James McNiesh for Lovelock.

For product information and technology assistance,
in Australia call **1300 790 853**;
in New Zealand call **0800 449 725**

For permission to use material from this text or product, please email **aust.permissions@cengage.com**

National Library of New Zealand Cataloguing-in-Publication Data
Thomas, Jenny, 1972-
Achievement English @ year 12 / Jenny Thomas and Diane White.
ISBN 9780170244213
1. English language—Rhetoric. 2. English language—Composition and exercises. I. White, Diane. II. Title.
808.042—dc 22

Cengage Learning Australia
Level 7, 80 Dorcas Street
South Melbourne, Victoria Australia 3205

Cengage Learning New Zealand
Unit 4B Rosedale Office Park
331 Rosedale Road, Albany, North Shore 0632, NZ

For learning solutions, visit **cengage.com.au**

Printed in China by China Translation & Printing Services.
1 2 3 4 5 6 7 16 15 14 13 12

Contents

1 Year 12. You've survived NCEA Level 1!

Last year, as you worked so hard to achieve NCEA Level 1, you acquired many of the crucial skills to make Year 12, Level 2, a great success too.

You've experienced external assessment now and you probably have a good idea of your own strengths and possible weaknesses. ***Achievement English @ Year 12*** is designed to help you extend your understanding of English texts while helping to improve skill areas that still need strengthening.

Things are going to be a little more sophisticated this time … both in what you are going to read/watch/listen to and how you are asked to respond to these different texts. Your teacher will expect you to demonstrate greater thinking skills and greater independence in your work habits. In ***Achievement English @ Year 12*** the advice and the exercises are designed to support and strengthen your skills in close reading, written expression and presentation.

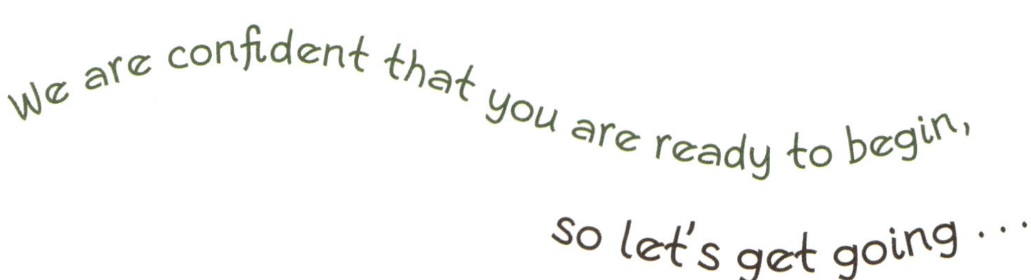

ISBN 9780170244213

2

Close Reading – learning to analyse significant aspects of unfamiliar text

In Year 12 you will be expected to read, understand and respond to unfamiliar text by:

- analysis
- interpretation
- evaluation

and to show your:

- understanding
- appreciation.

As you already know, a text might be a novel, a short story, a magazine article, a poem, a poster, a still from a film etc.

Familiarity with basic terminology is expected of you now. You know what a noun, a verb and an adjective is. You can recognise a simile, a metaphor or personification. This year you will be expected to focus more on the **effects** of a writer's choice of words, sentence structure and composition.

This greater focus on the reasons for a writer's use of language techniques, or a director's use of film techniques, acknowledges their careful, selective use of words and images. Nothing in a passage, a book, a film is accidental; every word, every frame is chosen with an effect on the reader or viewer in mind. A story for a five-year-old needs to use a very different vocabulary and syntax from that of a story for a teenager, just as a piece for the *TV Guide* will use a different language style and structure from an entry in a scientific journal.

Achievement English @ Year 12 is not designed solely for assessment. We are aiming to develop your understanding of, and ability to respond to, anything you read, see or hear. Think about it. Every day you read news or blogs on the internet; you hear opinion and lyrics on the radio; you browse through a magazine; you read a novel or a non-fiction book. Plus every other classroom you go into, with its posters and its text books, presents you with words and images to think about. Close reading is not restricted to assessment in English classes. It is a universal skill.

NCEA assessments will separate the close reading of unfamiliar written text (AS 2.3) from visual and oral text (AS 2.10).

Achievement English @ Year 12 helps you improve your close reading skills with a variety of texts. Use all the exercises, even if you are not taking one particular Achievement Standard. Keep the big picture in mind. ☺

There's a bigger picture … it's not just about assessment, it's everything out there!

ISBN 9780170244213

Check it!

By now you will be familiar with the basic terminology such as the recognition of parts and figures of speech that will already have been part of your study.

But just in case, let's work out what you do know as well as what you don't know. In this section you will be able to check your level of understanding of the terminology that you should already know from your study at Year 11.

Bonus points

Highlight and annotate an example of each of the following sentence types:

- *simple*
- *compound*
- *compound complex.*

Things to do with prose ...

The following is a short passage from Harper Lee's novel *To Kill a Mockingbird*. When you have read the passage, annotate each identified term.

proper noun

compound word

alliteration

adjective

noun

adverb

repetition

Maycomb was an old town, but it was a tired old town when I first knew it. In rainy weather the streets turned to red slop; grass grew on the sidewalks, the court-house sagged in the square. Somehow, it was hotter then; a black dog suffered on a summer's day; bony mules hitched to Hoover carts flicked flies in the sweltering shade of the live oaks on the square. Men's stiff collars wilted by nine in the morning. Ladies bathed before noon, after their three o'clock naps, and by nightfall were **like** soft teacakes with frostings of sweat and sweet talcum.

People moved slowly then. They ambled across the square, shuffled in and out of the stores around it, took their time about everything. A day was twenty-four hours long but seemed longer. There was **no** hurry, for there was **no**where to go, **nothing** to buy and **no** money to buy it with, **nothing** to see outside the boundaries of Maycomb County. But it was a time of vague optimism for some of the people; Maycomb County had recently been told that it had nothing to fear but fear itself.

personification

onomatopoeia

pronoun

simile

verb

conjunction

cliché

ISBN 9780170244213

Things to do with poetry ...

This is a popular poem by Ted Hughes. Read the poem carefully and then complete the task that follows.

The Jaguar

The apes yawn and adore their fleas in the sun.
The parrots shriek as if they were on fire, or strut
Like cheap tarts to attract the stroller with the nut.
Fatigued with indolence, tiger and lion

Lie still as the sun. The boa-constrictor's coil
Is a fossil. Cage after cage seems empty, or
Stinks of sleepers from the breathing straw.
It might be painted on a nursery wall.

But who runs like the rest past these arrives
At a cage where the crowd stands, stares, mesmerized,
As a child at a dream, at a jaguar hurrying enraged
Through prison darkness after the drills of his eyes

On a short fierce fuse. Not in boredom –
The eye satisfied to be blind in fire,
By the bang of blood in the brain deaf the ear –
He spins from the bars, but there's no cage to him

More than to the visionary his cell:
His stride is wildernesses of freedom:
The world rolls under the long thrust of his heel.
Over the cage floor the horizons come.

Ted Hughes

Find, highlight and annotate as many examples of the following as you can:

- ○ Simile
- ○ Metaphor
- ○ Personification
- ○ Alliteration
- ○ Onomatopoeia
- ○ Rhyme

ISBN 9780170244213

Things to do with visuals ...

Read the advertisement carefully and then complete the task that follows.

Find, highlight and annotate as many examples of the following as you can:

- ○ Headline
- ○ Body copy
- ○ Adjective/s
- ○ Alliteration
- ○ Compound word
- ○ Colloquial language
- ○ Cliché
- ○ Dominant visual feature
- ○ Emotive language
- ○ Imperative
- ○ Logos
- ○ Personal pronouns
- ○ Pun
- ○ Repetition
- ○ Slogan
- ○ Colour
- ○ Font (choice/ changes in)

So now you will be aware of any gaps in your knowledge. Fill them in by referring to the Language Lists at the back of this book. If you need more explanation, go back to your copy of ***Achievement English @ Year 11***. Alternatively we recommend ***Essential English*** for a comprehensive list of the technical terms used in the study of English.

ISBN 9780170244213

Close Reading – let's recap the basics

In this chapter our intention is to remind you of the essential elements of close reading:

- understanding the question fully
  and
- understanding the text fully.

The essentials

Let's consider some general questions you might be asked about any text that you are evaluating, whether it be familiar, unfamiliar, prose, poetry, oral or visual.

1 What is it about?

Essentially this question is asking for an explanation of the subject or topic of a piece. Is it a:

- work of fiction or fact?
- about a character?
- a place?
- an event?
- an object?

BUT what is it *really* about?

In the study of English the word **theme** or **idea** is often used, too. 'What is the theme of this text?' is a common question. Your answer should look more deeply at the text. For example, a short story might be 'about' a school trip to the ski field where an accident occurs, but on a deeper level its theme might be the recklessness of youth.

2 What is its purpose?

This question wants to know what (you think) the author's intention or purpose is. Purpose can be divided simply into categories like:

- to persuade
- to entertain
- to promote an action or thought
- to inform
- to amuse.

BUT often there is more than one purpose behind a text.

Writers sometimes want to change the way we see things, to make familiar things seem new. Writers of novels and short stories want to create believable characters with whom the reader can empathise and perhaps learn from. Or they want to give us new things to think about – science fiction writers may do this. Sometimes they want to share their experiences, for example in autobiographies, or persuade us into thinking the same way they do, for example, preachers and politicians.

When looking for a writer's purpose, especially in non-fiction, it is important to be able to differentiate between fact and opinion.

ISBN 9780170244213

3 What is its tone?

This question often troubles students but, when you think about it, you cope with tone every day of your life. Think of it as 'tone of voice'. Imagine your mother saying to you: 'Where have you been?' The importance of this question, and the way in which you respond to it, depends entirely on the way she has said it. Is she angry? Frustrated? Amused? Absent-minded? The only way to tell is by her tone of voice.

Try to use the same judgement on a written text. You might not have voice modulation to help you but you will have the clues through things like the writer's choice of words and sentence structure (syntax).

BUT, you may be asked about the writer or director's **style**.

The choice of vocabulary, sentence structure and figurative language each contribute to creating the style of a text. For example, it may be a spare, minimalist passage describing a man in a prison camp, or a flowery romantic description of a teenage girl falling in love.

4 Who is the intended audience?

We are used to the word 'audience' meaning those who watch a film or see a play performed on stage. Where written text is concerned 'audience' means readers.

This question wants to know what kind of person you think the piece has been written/produced for. Sometimes it will be for a very specific type of person, for example a beginning reader will be aimed at five-year-olds or an advertisement for a new performance by a ballet company will be aimed at those who enjoy ballet. Sometimes it will be for a very wide group, for example: the front page article in a daily newspaper will be aimed at everyone over the age of 12 who reads the news; or a biography on Dan Carter would be aimed at anyone who enjoys reading about rugby and famous people.

BUT, some things can appeal to different audiences on different levels.

For example, a comic show for small children may well contain some jokes for adults that the children will not understand.

An aside on ... voice/point of view

Has the writer created a persona? Is the writer giving his or her own opinion or are they putting words in another person's mouth? Is the writer's opinion clear, even when a persona is being used?

A writer of fiction may use characters to voice opinions other than their own. An editor of a newspaper may be voicing the paper's opinion (or its owner's), not their own.

ISBN 9780170244213

Take note!

When you are really trying to understand a text it can help to make detailed notes, around the words if it is a written text, as you read it several times. This is called **annotation**.

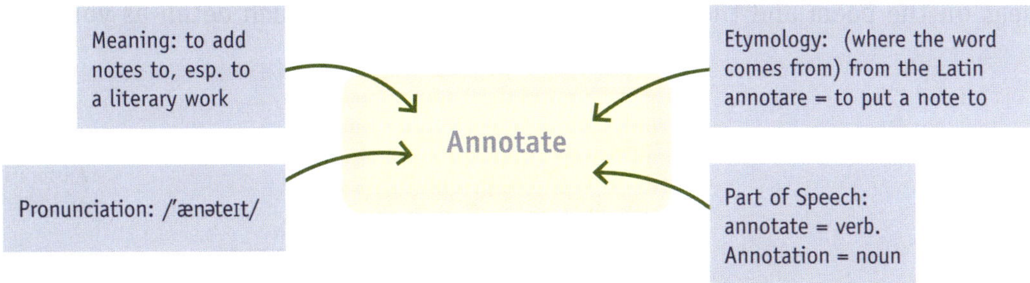

Why annotate?

To help us make complete sense of the passage.

What to annotate?

- explanations of words you needed to look up in a dictionary
- figurative language like similes and metaphors
- effective vocabulary
- details that may answer specific questions
- links between different parts of the text
- anything you see as interesting/important.

What to do with the annotations?

After this 'technical read', look at how these things you have noted work for the passage as a whole. Are they building an image of a character? Is a setting being created? Are they giving the reader a specific mood or atmosphere?

At Year 12 you will be asked to look at the total effect of a text more often that ever before. It may help to try and put yourself in the shoes of the writer and work out why you might have chosen those specific words.

If you find it difficult to get started, try this format:

Read once

- Read passage/poem quietly to yourself.

Read twice

- Read the passage/poem again.
- Check you understand the vocabulary. Do you know what all the words mean?
- Highlight words you don't understand and use a dictionary to give you clear, appropriate meanings.
- Write these definitions on the page.

Read again

- Highlight and annotate any figurative language.
- Note other effective words and phrases.
- Note any special sentence structures.
- What do these things add to your understanding?
- Think about the tone created in the passage. How is it created?
- Is there a particular style? How is it created?

ISBN 9780170244213

Putting all this into practice

Let's look closely at one short poem written by the famous poet, W.H. Auden.

Use all of these suggestions to help you fully understand and appreciate the text.

Read our annotations, adding any of your own. Use the boxes provided to help you organise your ideas on the poem and then answer the questions in as much detail as you can.

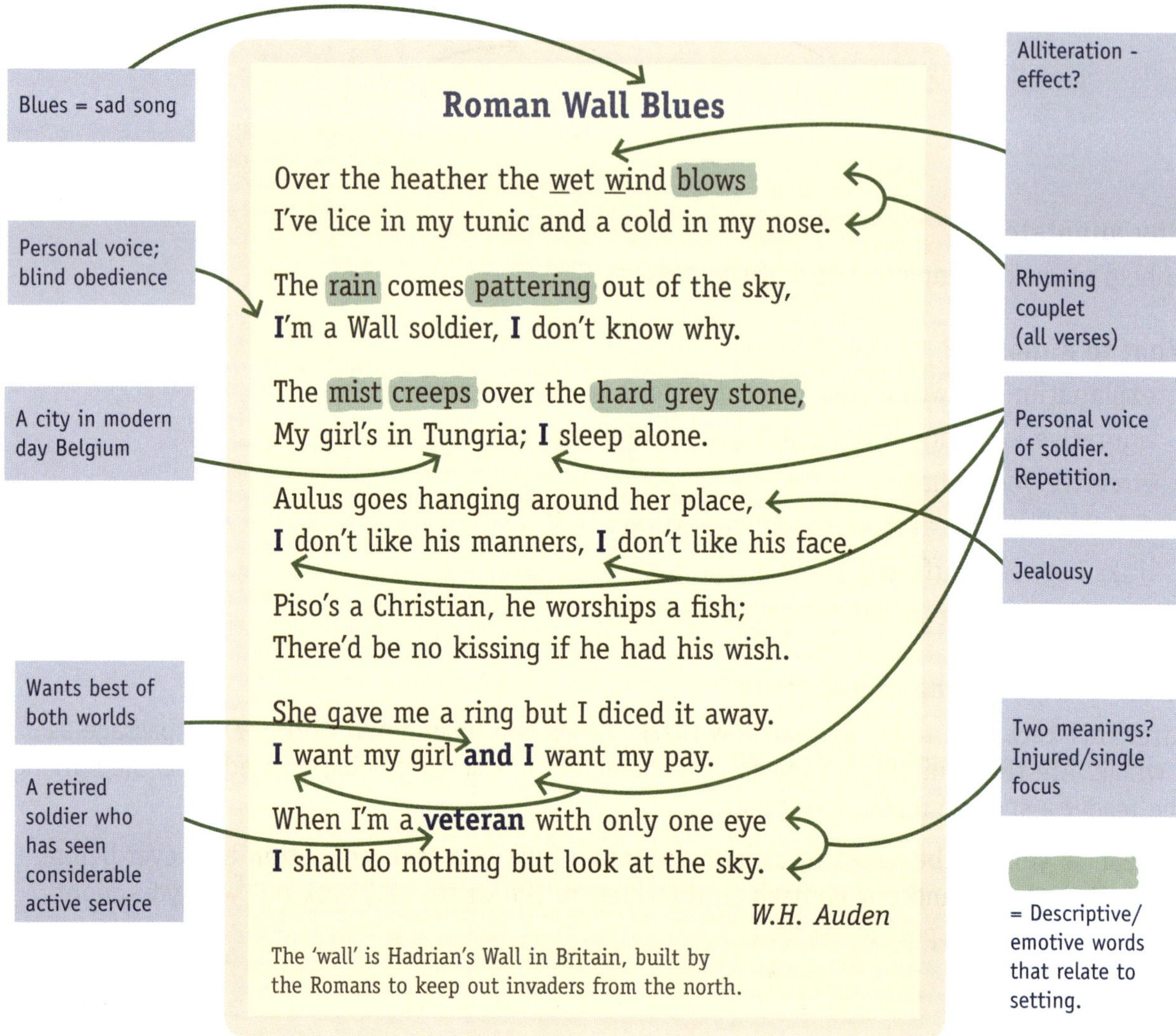

Roman Wall Blues

Over the heather the wet wind blows
I've lice in my tunic and a cold in my nose.

The rain comes pattering out of the sky,
I'm a Wall soldier, I don't know why.

The mist creeps over the hard grey stone,
My girl's in Tungria; I sleep alone.

Aulus goes hanging around her place,
I don't like his manners, I don't like his face.

Piso's a Christian, he worships a fish;
There'd be no kissing if he had his wish.

She gave me a ring but I diced it away.
I want my girl **and** I want my pay.

When I'm a **veteran** with only one eye
I shall do nothing but look at the sky.

W.H. Auden

The 'wall' is Hadrian's Wall in Britain, built by the Romans to keep out invaders from the north.

Before you go further ...

Complete the following chart.

What is it **about**?	Who is the **audience**?	What is the **style**?	What is the **purpose**?

ISBN 9780170244213

Answer the following questions in as much detail as possible:

1 What is the poem about?

2 What is the poet's purpose?

3 What is the poem's tone?

4 Who is the intended audience?

5 What is the attitude of the writer?

1 What is the poem about?

The poem is giving the thoughts of a soldier in a Roman legion who is guarding a border. He is describing the conditions he is working in, his longing for home, and his hopes for his future.

2 What is the poet's purpose?

The poet is using the first person 'I' to suggest the poem is being expressed by the soldier and through him the poet is commenting on the conditions of soldiers, and showing that they do not think about what or who they are fighting for, 'I'm a Wall soldier, I don't know why', they just think about their personal circumstances, like this soldier who is worried about his girlfriend.

3 What is the poem's tone?

The tone of this poem is one of complaint. He is miserable about the lice and the cold, he is lonely: 'I want my girl'. He is longing for a better life: 'I shall do nothing'.

4 Who is the intended audience?

This poem is written to illustrate to the general public that soldiers are real people and do not enjoy their work. It also makes a comment on soldiers generally, in that they do not know why they are fighting. The poet's intended audience is anyone who is interested in the reality of war, in this case one in the past.

5 What is the attitude of the writer?

The writer is sympathetic towards the soldier and his situation. He tells us, through the soldier's eyes, all that is wrong with his job: the boredom, the discomfort, the loneliness and the lack of rewards. He does not suggest any purpose for a man in this role.

ISBN 9780170244213

Digging deeper

In Year 12 the texts you study will be more sophisticated than those you read or watched or listened to in Year 11. The notes you make will also be more extensive. Here we provide sample annotations for a more sophisticated text.

These are the opening paragraphs of the novel *Shipping News* by Annie Proulx. It is a complex piece of writing and to understand it well you need to read it with great care. The annotations will help you appreciate the writing. Use them to answer the question that follows.

The paragraphs have been annotated for you to show how a student can focus on effective vocabulary, figurative language, deeper meaning etc.

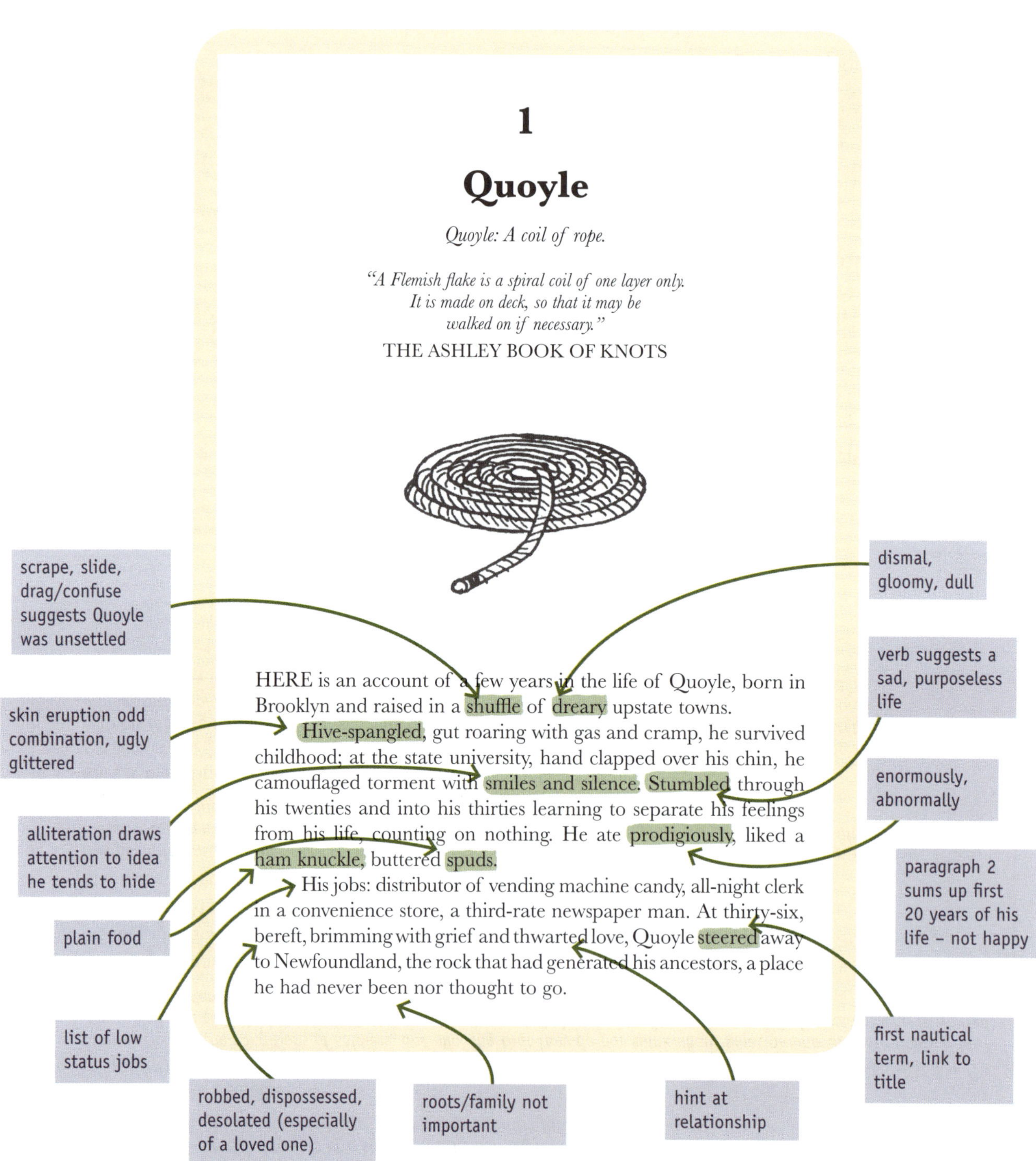

ISBN 9780170244213

A watery place. And Quoyle feared water, could not swim. Again and again the father had broken his clenched grip and thrown him into pools, brooks, lakes and surf. Quoyle knew the flavour of brack and waterweed.

From this youngest son's failure to dog-paddle the father saw other failures multiply like an explosion of virulent cells—failure to speak clearly; failure to sit up straight; failure to get up in the morning; failure in attitude; failure in ambition and ability; indeed in everything. His own failure.

Quoyle shambled, a head taller than any child around him, was soft. He knew it. 'Ah, you lout,' said the father. But no pygmy himself. And brother Dick, the father's favorite, pretended to throw up when Quoyle came into a room, hissed 'Lardass, Snotface, Ugly Pig, Warthog, Stupid, Stinkbomb, Fart-tub, Greasebag,' pummelled and kicked until Quoyle curled, hands over head, snivelling, on the linoleum. All stemmed from Quoyle's chief failure, a failure of normal appearance.

A great damp loaf of a body. At six he weighed eighty pounds. At sixteen he was buried under a casement of flesh. Head shaped like a crenshaw, no neck, reddish hair ruched back. Features as bunched as kissed fingertips. Eyes the color of plastic. The monstrous chin, a freakish shelf jutting from the lower face.

Some anomalous gene had fired up at the moment of his begetting as a single spark sometimes leaps from banked coals, had given him a giant's chin. As a child he invented stratagems to deflect stares; a smile, a downcast gaze, the right hand darting up to cover the chin.

His earliest sense of self was as a distant figure: there in the foreground was his family; here, at the limit of the far view, was he. Until he was fourteen he cherished the idea that he had been given to the wrong family, that somewhere his real people, saddled with the changeling of the Quoyles, longed for him. Then, foraging in a box of excursion mementoes, he found photographs of his father beside brothers and sisters at a ship's rail. A girl, somewhat apart from the others, looked towards the sea, eyes squinted, as though she could see the port of destination a thousand miles south. Quoyle recognised himself in their hair, their legs and arms.

Annotations:

- not 'his' father – suggests distance lack of love?
- hard consonants, suggests cruelty?
- list – shows the many times he had been thrown into water
- father blaming son? minor sentence. Makes idea notable
- repetition of failure, Quoyle's parent's accusations
- simile
- does not retaliate – cruel father, brother
- poisonous, malignant
- metaphor – rising dough
- suggesting he is criticised in such a hostile way because he looks different
- simile – squashed face. Ugly
- means frame of a window. Buried – his real self is hidden under his appearance
- no colour (no spirit?)
- adjectives suggest abnormal, absurd, inhuman
- in folds
- metaphor
- feels unwanted, unloved by his family

1 Using the information you have gleaned from the annotated notes on pages 14/15, answer this question in as much detail as possible:

How has the writer introduced the main character, Quoyle, in the opening paragraphs of this novel? Consider setting (time, place, social background) and character (appearance, self-image, history etc). Look again at the quotation from *The Ashley Book of Knots*. Which words might apply to Quoyle?

An aside on ... using quotations

When you wish to use a quotation from a text use inverted commas (double or single is acceptable; just be consistent) to show the exact words you have copied. If you miss any words out, to shorten the quotation perhaps, then use ellipsis marks (...) to show where the gap is. For example:

Quoyle's brother seems to hate him. He 'hisses' at Quoyle, calling him horrible names like 'Lardass, Snotface ... Greasebag'.

ISBN 9780170244213

Let's go a step further...

Use the same annotating technique to examine the beginning of this short story *The Widow* by Maurice Gee. Significant words, phrases, sentences have been underlined or highlighted for you. Try to identify the language techniques and more importantly the effect of the words used. If you imagine what is happening you will appreciate the piece more fully. Then answer the questions that follow using quotations from the text to support your points.

On a stinging-hot Boxing Day Phil Welch came to a neglected farm. The service-car's dust swirled in front of his eyes as he bent to find the name on the letter-box. But the box was grey and blank. Drawn apart by sun, showing lengths of rusty nail, it perched on a fence-post in wrinkled, shrugging hopelessness. Phil banged it affectionately. He had known this farm six years ago. The box was the same. It meant that most other things would be the same, his uncle and aunt in particular. There would be no work to do on this holiday.

He hefted his suitcase and started up the looping hillside road. By the time he had come down the other side to the house his clothes were sticking to him and sweat was stinging his eyes. Thankfully he lowered the case on to the bottom step, and took out his handkerchief. Mae came on to the porch. She put her hands on her hips and laughed at him. Yes, Mae, he thought hazily. Just the same. Still laughing. Probably still a little drunk — tiddly, as she called it: the untidy centre of the farm. He wiped his forehead and grinned up at her.

'Home in a canter,' she chuckled.

He went up the stairs and kissed her. 'Hello, Mae.'

Her eyes searched his face mockingly. She shook her head and laughed. 'Aren't we a big boy now.' He laughed too, delighted to find her unchanged — to find her still on the bottle. Her breath smelled of beer and her lower eyelids were loose, right-angled, each holding a little pool of water.

'Well,' she said, taking his arm, 'and what did he bring his old auntie for Christmas?' She gave him a wide smile, and he saw from the way the skin of her face slid to new places how loose it was; and her hair was a waxen colour, whitish-yellow, the colour of old men's moustaches. She was really growing old then? It gave him a little shock and he turned her quickly into the kitchen. There he slammed his case on the table, sprang its locks, and said, 'Close your eyes.'

Her red thick-fingered hands splashed across her face. 'It better be good.'

Quickly he dug into his clothes and unwrapped three bottles of wine. He stood them on the table. 'They're all yours,' he said.

ISBN 9780170244213

Answer the following questions in as much detail as possible:

1 What is the setting (time, place, social background) of this story?

2 What kind of person is Mae?

3 How does the young man, Phil, feel about this place and these people?

ISBN 9780170244213

Answering the question

The end result of much of your close reading at this level is to:

- have information to offer in a class discussion

  or
- answer questions – usually in writing.

Involving yourself in class discussion is an excellent way to improve your understanding of a text. We do appreciate, though, that writing answers to questions is usually where your results come from, so let's think about the question for a moment.

The most important thing is to make sure that you understand what the question is asking you to write. After all, there isn't much point filling up the allocated lines but not actually giving the information the examiner requires.

Here's a straightforward method for approaching the question/instruction:

1 Read it carefully, more than once.

2 Highlight/underline the key words. There may be more than one. Describe, explain, analyse, compare, contrast etc.

3 Plan your answer before you begin to write it.

   i This may involve going back to the text to re-read the part/s that are specifically referenced in the question (perhaps with a line or paragraph number) – and the part/s of the text around that reference.

   ii It may involve re-reading parts of the text where you think the answer is located.

   iii It will involve re-reading!

4 If you are asked several questions, with a few lines for each answer, these require shorter, more focused responses, and can sometimes be easier to answer, as they are more direct. You will see clearly what the examiner requires of you.

*Here's an easy way of thinking about questions. Remember who, what, where, when, why and how? Now the: who, what, where and when is the background information and the **WHY** and **HOW** are the really important questions.*

5 If you are given a longer question and a larger allocation of lines and you are expected to write an answer that is more in the style of an essay, don't panic! Generally these questions give you plenty of clues. Identify the different parts of the question so that you answer all the parts in your response. You might even highlight the different parts of the question to be really clear that you have understood the whole thing.

6 The way you answer questions will determine the mark you receive. If you answer a question in detail and support your ideas about the text with appropriate references and quotations you will reach Merit or Excellence level.

7 It is most important to offer personal responses that relate to your own life and experiences if you are asked. Always try to think about how the topic or theme of a text relates to real life ... your own life or life you observe around you.

ISBN 9780170244213

Let's have a look at a passage together

Read this excerpt from a magazine article and answer the questions that follow. We suggest that you read and annotate the passage several times before you begin to answer the questions.

CHE'S WAY

THERE'S MORE TO CHE FU, THE GODFATHER OF NEW ZEALAND HIP-HOP, THAN FAST TALK AND ATTITUDE. GINNY ANDERSON MET THE SINGER WITH THE MELLIFLUOUS VOICE AND SEVEN NUMBER ONE SINGLES.

THROW ALL YOUR PRE-CONCEPTIONS out the door. Forget what you thought you knew about hip-hop – like that LA gangster, ratbag in da hood, tough guy spinning rhymes of guns, women and violence thing. Che Fu is New Zealand's top hip-hop artist and one our most awarded musicians, and he's got there by changing the way Kiwis see hip-hop. The Che Fu I met on a humid afternoon in Auckland was no gangster – in fact, he was a gentleman.

Che Fu is a proud, 28-year-old father and husband who sings like a choir boy and raps like a poet. The soulful tunes he produces with lyrics espousing brotherhood, love and peace in a multi-cultural land have you grooving rather than grimacing. Che calls it 'conscious hip-hop'.

'We don't like the gangster stuff either; it's not helping anyone. It's only saleable because it's explicit.' Che says as we chat in his humble, Grey Lynn bungalow. His voice is soft, rhythmic. He believes the red warning stickers that appear on the covers of these CDs are like honey to the bee of angst-ridden teenagers, which is why this type of hip-hop is zealously promoted by record company executives. The result? Hip-hop gets a bad name, and Che wants that to change.

Then there's the confusion over what hip-hop really is. Isn't it an American thing? 'It's really a group of street arts – and it includes rapping, graffiti art, breakdancing and DJing. 'The latter two now have international competitions, says Che. 'You could say country music is 'American' and that's big here too. It's just a way of delivery.' Hip-hop Che-style all began when the fresh-faced boy of Niuean and Maori descent was introduced to New Zealand in 1995 as frontman and lead singer for trailblazing Kiwi ban, Supergroove 'You got to know to understand' were the lyrics on the lips of every music-loving teenager. A world tour at the age of 16 with the group (which began as a school band) was to be the beginning of an exciting musical career.

Che said goodbye to Supergroove in 1996 and embarked on his solo career. Seven number one singles, male vocalist of the year three times over, 1999 Rising Entertainer Prize and number two New Zealand album of the century behind Split Enz in a music magazine poll. Che's voice is mellifluous, angelic, somehow soothing. It's no wonder the awards have flowed. Reviewers have often described it as the best voice in New Zealand pop history. With that in mind, I asked if it's the singing that he enjoys most? His eyes light up. 'There's nothing better than getting up on the stage and performing. It helps when your band members are good mates,' he grins. However, this affinity with performing is surprising because in person Che appears shy, but perhaps he's just a man of few words and chooses them well.

His distinctive voice has given his second album, The Navigator, a soulful flavour and it's worked a treat with the fans. It entered the charts at number one in August last year and remained there for three consecutive weeks. Sony, his new recording label, has realised it could well have hot export property on its hands. So there's the tour to Australia this month to release the album there, then Che, his family , and his band, The Krates, head to London for another release tour.

Che's wife, Ange, is excited at the prospect, having never travelled to Europe. I asked about the kids. It doesn't seem to faze either of them. 'We'll be like the hip-hop Partridge family,' laughs Che. 'I can't understand musicians who travel the world and leave their wives and families behind. You'd have to ask why – you'd only do that if you wanted to get up to something.'

Che's more focused with making music and ensuring his family are happy and, of course, he's hopeful The Navigator will be well received aboard. Inspired musically and lyrically by his love of reggae, funk, soul and rap, it's an album that has wide appeal. Sony has described it as 'hip-hop with a chewy centre.' Put simple, it's music you can drive to – for hours (and it won't drive you barmy) – chill to, wiggle to, ponder over. And I can testify that you can even write to these serene tunes.

Perhaps fatherhood has influenced the album, I suggest, referring to its softness. 'It's not something I consciously think about,' says Che. But he admits life as certainly changed since embarking

ISBN 9780170244213

on a rock 'n' roll career at the age of 14. He's got a family to consider these days. There's smiling Ange, heavily pregnant with baby number two, and bright-eyed Loxmyn, his three-year-old son sporting traditional Nuiean black braids and a cheeky grin. Che says he's more likely to be playing with his son in the backyard than chasing fame. 'Music is how I feed my family. To me, success isn't about MTV.'

Family and music have always been of the essence. Born Che Ness in Auckland's Ponsonby – at a time when you'd be more likely to find Polynesian markets than cafes, bars and fashion stores - he was brought up in 'a cultural melting pot'. But the Polynesian culture was significant in shaping his musical talent. Particularly the oral tradition, the singing and dancing.

His father's love of reggae meant Che also grew up with Bob Marley. 'We could relate to reggae. It spoke for the poor people, the ghetto people – the music said something about the truth.' He reflects somberly. Bob still looks over Che today, from a faded poster in his garden studio. Affectionately known as the Chop Shop, this prefab nestled directly under Auckland's North Western motorway is where Che produces and writes his music in the dead of the night, when it's as quiet as it gets.

It smells like rock 'n' roll, cigarettes and sweat. He shows me his sampler, the piece of equipment responsible for all those quirky sounds. Somehow Che manages to put the beeps, raps and taps into some semblance. 'It must take you hours to pieces a track together,' I say. Che looks back knowingly and nods.

Another tool that pulls the music together is the sound-mix programme on Che's heavy-duty computer. But it's not all bells and whistles. There's still a good old guitar poked in the corner and a couple of turntables, of course. A more unusual addition to the Chop Shop is the shelf stuffed with plastic Star Wars figurines. He's a pop-culture pack rat – you get the feeling he's still a big kid.

It's not all about music then? Che's eyes wander at the suggestion. He's mad on Manga comics, and he dabbles in animation, but then he's back talking about music. 'I like to scratch. It's great for stress relief.' No idea what scratching is? Imagine someone on a set of turntables scratching the needle back and forth over the vinyl to make, well, scratching noises – it's a DJ/hip-hop thing.

Video production is another feather in Che's cap. 'Not by choice, he says. It's the only way he can control the end product. 'Let's just say I'm an insecure person,' he laughs. On a more serious note, 'I've got to remember I also represent my mum, my dad, my aunties. I represent the Pacific Nation, indigenous people.'

So you can see why Che wants to get it right. He wants to make a positive impression on the people who listen to his music. He would like to spread the good word about this country and its people. 'We live in a small, isolated country, but we're on the cutting edge of technology – we're practical people able to solve problems without waiting around for someone else to help us. I can drive for 30 minutes and be alone in a forest. New Zealand is on the outside looking in and that's what gives us a clearer view of the world.'

On the flipside, Che hopes his music will give the rest of the world a clearer view of New Zealand and its people. The one thing he recalls vividly from that first word tour was the surprise on people's faces on the street. 'They'd never seen a Polynesian face like mine before. They were like, 'Where do you come from?' That seems set to change if Che's impending European tour goes to plan.

I wave Che and the hip-hop Partridge family goodbye, then head back to the office. While trying to pen a few words about what conscious hip-hop means, I subconsciously tune in to his CD playing in the office. The lyrics from 'Misty Frequencies', the first track on The Navigator encapsulates the idea better than I can. It says: 'More than sound. More than words. Must be keeping them healthy. What you hear what you see ain't always what it's supposed to be. We tune down real slow. Searching on the hi-fi radio. For something with that feeling. We alive again.' Ⓟ

ISBN 9780170244213

Although a final assessment will not use marks in the way we have used them here, it also will not use questions that are so tightly focused as these are. We have allocated marks for this exercise so that you can see how marks (and therefore grades) are built up through detailed answers to questions.

1 Identify and explain **three** ways in which the writer involves the reader/audience in the first paragraph.

i ______

ii ______

iii ______

(2 marks)

2 A simile is used in paragraph 3. Identify it and explain its effect.

______

______

______

______

(2 marks)

3 Explain the writer's attitude towards record company executives expressed in paragraph 3.

______

______

______

______

(2 marks)

4 Che claims to represent New Zealand and Polynesia. What is the basis for this claim?

______

______

______

(2 marks)

5 In paragraph 4 why does the writer use a question?

______

______

______

(1 mark)

6 What purpose do the brackets in line 23 have?

______

______

______

(1 mark)

ISBN 9780170244213

7 What part of speech is the word 'trailblazing' (paragraph 4)? What does it mean in this context?

____

____

(2 marks)

8 Paragraphs 5 and 10 each contain a minor sentence. Give the first and last words of each one.

i ____

ii ____

(1 mark)

9 Identify as many links between the verbal and visual features of this article as possible.

____

____

____

____

____

____

____

____

(3 marks)

10 Select five adjectives used to describe Che's voice. What is the writer suggesting about Che's music by using these words?

i ________________ ii ________________ iii ________________

iv ________________ v ________________

Explanation ____________________________________

____

____

(2 marks)

11 At whom is the article aimed? How can you tell? Quote evidence from the text.

____

____

____

____

____

(2 marks)

Total 

ISBN 9780170244213

Below you will find an example of how another Year 12 student tackled this work. The student's answers have been marked with the marker's comments. Read them carefully with reference to your own answers.

1 Identify and explain **three** ways in which the writer involves the reader/audience in the first paragraph.

(2 marks)

The writer involves the reader by:

i) Using personal pronouns – 'Forget what you thought you knew…' – which makes the reader feel directly linked, as if he/she is being talked to as an individual.

1 mark The technique is identified, an accurate example given and the effect explained.

ii) Using colloquial language – 'ratbag in da hood' – which is used to appeal to the teenage generation.

0 marks This language is slang, not colloquial. Also the article is not aimed primarily at teenagers. A better answer would identify the slang and explain how the writer uses it to introduce the subject, to give the reader some reference points.

iii) Using the word 'Kiwis' and local place name 'Auckland', which a New Zealand reader would relate to.

1 mark This answer is sufficient. The student might also have mentioned use of the imperatives 'Throw' and 'Forget' which instruct the reader and thus involve him/her. Note that the material chosen MUST be from the first paragraph only. The student receives only one mark because they did not provide three satisfactory responses.

2 A simile is used in paragraph 3. Identify it and explain its effect.

(2 marks)

'red warning stickers … are like honey to the bee'. This simile shows how quickly explicit lyrics sell to teenagers.

1 mark The simile is correctly identified (note that the student has given both sides of the comparison). The student needed to make reference to the strong natural attraction that the writer is suggesting naughty/forbidden/anti-social lyrics seem to have for teenagers by choosing this comparison.

ISBN 9780170244213

3 Explain the writer's attitude towards record company executives expressed in paragraph 3.

(3 marks)

He is showing that the record companies only care about whether it sells, not about the actual music or its effects. Record companies are irresponsible for selling dirty demerit explicit albums to kids just for the high turnover.

2 marks This answer is sufficient. It gives an opinion (irresponsible) and an accurate explanation. It fails to mention the destruction of hip-hop's reputation, which would have given an additional mark.

4 Che claims to represent New Zealand and Polynesia. What is the basis for this claim?

(1 mark)

'Niuean and Maori descent' – he is part Polynesian and part Maori and represents them both.

1 mark Explaining that Niue is a Pacific Island and Maori are New Zealanders would be appropriate here if more than 1 mark were allocated to the question.

5 In paragraph 4 why does the writer use a question?

(1 mark)

He uses a question that might be used by the reader, in rhetorical form, and then gives the correct answer and clears up any misconceptions the reader might have about hip-hop.

1 mark The student could have mentioned that giving the question introduces Che's own interpretation of the genre.

6 What purpose do the brackets in line 23 have?

(1 mark)

They show additional information that is not needed to make the sentence make sense. We do not need to know how his band started but it is interesting to know that he started out small.

1 mark This is a full response explaining the use of parentheses.

ISBN 9780170244213

7 What part of speech is the word 'trail-blazing'? What does it mean in this context?

(2 marks)

Popular, many people followed.

0 marks This is not a clear enough response. Answering in note form is not recommended. For this question the student needs to answer both elements of the question. The word is used as an adjective. It means the group was making new music, doing things never done before but copied afterwards.

8 Paragraphs 5 and 10 each contain a minor sentence. Give the first and last words of each one.

(1 mark)

i) Seven ... poll.

ii) Particularly ... dancing.

1 mark Each sentence identified has no completed verb.

9 Identify as many links between the verbal and visual features of this article as possible.

(3 marks)

a) How happy he looks, smiling and relaxed – 'Che is a ... proud father and husband.' – He is clearly happy with his life.

b) The casual boyish way he is dressed – 'you get the feeling he's stilla big kid'.

c) The article is about a musician and the picture has a guitar, a sampler, guitar and turntable, all of which are mentioned in the text.

3 marks Each point is made separately and refers both to text and to the image. There are other points that could be made, for example the article focuses on Che and he is pictured; it talks about the Chop Shop studio and this is where the photograph is taken. The crowded unimposing studio is referred to and the picture has Che in a corner, surrounded by equipment with bare pipes showing. This image also reinforces the lack of interest in material things he expresses. Note that the question asks for several links and is worth three marks. Giving at least three examples is therefore indicated.

ISBN 9780170244213

10 Select five adjectives used to describe Che's voice. What is the writer suggesting about Che's music by using these words?

(2 marks)

i) mellifluous ii) soulful iii) soft iv) rhythmic v) angelic

It is not as harsh as usual hip-hop, he has made it soulful. Is calming and has its own style.

2 marks The student has correctly identified five adjectives and explained that this is not what you might expect from hip-hop.

11 At whom is the article aimed? How can you tell? Quote evidence from the text.

(2 marks)

Teenagers. It uses colloquial language for teenagers, gangsta, hip-hop, scratching.

0 marks Incorrect identification of audience and incorrectly identifies slang as colloquial language.

The article is aimed at an older audience: adults interested in music but not very knowledgeable about young music. It explains 'scratching', as 'imagine someone on a set of turntables ...', invites the reader to 'throw all your preconceptions out the door' and adults are more likely to have preconceptions about hip-hop than teenagers are. It calls teenagers 'angst ridden', which an article aimed at teenagers would not, and it focuses a lot on the devoted family man – 'Music is how I feed my family. To me success isn't about MTV' – which would appeal more to adults.

Overall a sound response to a variety of question types.

Now go back to your own answers and see how they compare with the answers given here. NCEA assessment may not be as focused as these questions. Remember, ***Achievement English @ Year 12*** is helping you prepare for assessment by practising close reading approaches.

An aside on ... answering the question too soon

One common error that students make is rushing into writing an answer before they are really ready. Reading the passage through once quickly and rushing on to the questions is not a good idea.

Many students assume that because the marks come from the answers to questions then that is the most important part of the process. Wrong! Understanding the text fully and thinking about the answer carefully before putting pen to paper (or fingers to keyboard) is where you lay the foundation of your marks.

If you are given a set time to complete a close reading exercise, we suggest using a good half of that time to read and understand the text, and prepare notes on your answers. Try it, it works ...

READ ANNOTATE THINK PREPARE WRITE

ISBN 9780170244213

Just one more thing ...

Achievement English @ Year 12 continues to help develop your strategies for close reading unfamiliar text. We have used a variety of increasingly sophisticated types of both texts and questions to help you increase your own confidence in your close reading skills. We have given you opportunities to practise identifying key style features and explain how and why the author chose to use them. We expect you to be familiar with essential language terms, and their definitions, so you will be able to use them with authority as you explain what you understand about the texts.

You will now have met the term 'scaffolded question'. You will recollect that a 'scaffold' is a support structure, usually around a building being developed. However, when talking about a scaffolded question in English it refers to a question that offers you support, or hints, as to how to answer the question. Such a question will demand a longer, more detailed and self-structured answer.

This takes more effort, especially in planning your answer.

Scaffolded questions will not ask about an isolated technique or meaning or purpose. Instead, they will ask a wider question but will give you ideas about how to answer them in depth and detail.

Always use the clues to complete your answer ☺

So what does this mean?

- Instead of being given several short, specific questions you are given one or two more general questions.
- These questions demand a longer, more structured answer.
- You may be given a few ideas about what you might include in your answer.

Is that important?

- Your answer will be assessed as N, A, M, or E depending on the detail in the response you provide.
- Show that you have heeded the advice you have been given by planning your answer carefully using that advice.
- Your aim is a response that clearly expresses your understanding of the text.

ISBN 9780170244213

Here is an example of the kind of question we are talking about:

Analyse how the writer creates an informal tone to connect with the reader. In your answer you should:

- identify and give examples of **techniques** used in the text, and explain their **effects** (techniques might include word choice, contrast, and narrative style)
- show understanding of the ideas the writer is communicating show understanding of the writer's **overall purpose**.

This question gives you a clear indication of how the answer should be structured to include at least the three techniques named, and to then you go on to reveal your understanding of the purpose of the passage and how that identified tone suits that identified purpose.

How do you tackle this kind of question?

Like any other question you are asked!

You are used to answering very specific short questions relating to text. *Why is the word 'xxx' used? What does this metaphor suggest?* etc These answers are very similar, they are usually just asking you to think about the text as a whole.

As with any other question, the key thing is that you actually answer the question. Don't worry about the string of empty lines below the question that you feel have to fill with writing.

Use this strategy to help you:

- Read the question twice.
- Underline key words.
- Read and re-read the passage.
- Underline or highlight detail that looks important to you as you go.
- Go back to the hints or bullet points.
- Check if there's anything else in the passage you want to highlight.
- Take a few minutes to plan your answer. Think of it as a small essay.
- Make sure you are using specific language terms if possible.
- Check that you always support any point you make with an example.
- Write your answer.
- Re-read your answer – **have you answered the question?**

ISBN 9780170244213

Let's look at a question together

Let's look closely at a poem written by RS Thomas. Read our annotations, adding any of your own, to help you fully understand and appreciate the text. Then answer the questions in as much detail as you can.

Cynddylan on a Tractor

Ah, you should see Cynddylan on a tractor,
Gone the old look that yoked him to the soil;
He's a new man now, part of the machine,
His nerves of metal and his blood oil.
The clutch curses, but the gears obey
His least bidding, and lo, he's away
Out of the farmyard, scattering hens.
Riding to work now as a great man should,
He is the knight at arms breaking the fields'
Mirror of silence, emptying the wood
Of foxes and squirrels and bright jays.
The sun comes over the tall trees
Kindling all the hedges, but not for him
Who runs his engine on a different fuel.
And all the birds are singing, bills wide in vain,
As Cynddylan passes proudly up the lane.

RS Thomas

Cynddylan is the name of a legendary heroic Welsh ruler.

Exclamations = be amazed.

Interesting word choice. Means 'tied to'.

Personification. He's not a good driver but he is in charge of the tractor.

Metaphors. He loves the new machine. He feels heroic riding it.

Alliteration 'k' sound like the noise of the clutch grinding.

Verbs suggesting negative effect on natural world.

Simile shows he sits high and proud.

The creatures fleeing from the machine, overwhelmed by it.

No use, he cannot hear the natural world.

Alliteration. Passes sounds quite regal and proudly also links to idea of his own importance.

ISBN 9780170244213

Answer the following questions in as much detail as possible. The annotations around the poem will help you scaffold your answers.

1 In Welsh legend Cynddylan was a celebrated heroic ruler. How does the poet suggest Cynddylan feels like a hero?

2 How has this new possession altered Cynddylan's relationship with nature?

ISBN 9780170244213

Before you go further

Now it is time for you to have a go on your own. Below are the opening paragraphs from *Bleak House* by Charles Dickens. Read the passage at least twice, annotating important features.

In Chancery*

London. Michaelmas term lately over, and the Lord Chancellor sitting in Lincoln's Inn Hall. Implacable November weather. As much mud in the streets, as if the waters had but newly retired from the face of the earth, and it would not be wonderful to meet a Megalosaurus, forty feet long or so, waddling like an elephantine lizard up Holborn Hill. Smoke lowering down from chimney-pots, making a soft black drizzle with flakes of soot in it as big as full-grown snowflakes – gone into mourning, one might imagine, for the death of the sun. Dogs, undistinguishable in mire. Horses scarcely better; splashed to their very blinkers. Foot passengers, jostling one another's umbrellas, in a general infection of ill temper, and losing their foot-hold at street-corners, where tens of thousands of other foot passengers have been slipping and sliding since the day broke (if this day ever broke), adding new deposits to the crust upon crust of mud, sticking at those points tenaciously to the pavement, and accumulating at compound interest.

Fog everywhere. Fog up the river, where it flows among green aits and meadows; fog down the river, where it rolls defiled among the tiers of shipping, and the waterside pollutions of a great (and dirty) city. Fog on the Essex Marshes, fog on the Kentish heights. Fog creeping into the cabooses of collier brigs; fog lying out on the yards, and hovering in the rigging of great ships; fog drooping on the gunwales of barges and small boats. Fog in the eyes and throats of ancient Greenwich pensioners, wheezing by the firesides of their wards; fog in the stem and bowl of the afternoon pipe of the wrathful skipper, down in his close cabin; fog cruelly pinching the toes and fingers of his shivering little 'prentice boy on deck. Chance people on the bridges peeping over the parapets into a nether sky of fog, with fog all around them, as if they were up in a balloon, and hanging in the misty clouds.

Gas looming through the fog in divers places in the streets, much as the sun may, from the spongy fields, be seen to loom by husbandman and ploughboy. Most of the shops lighted two hours before their time – as the gas seems to know, for it has a haggard and unwilling look.

The raw afternoon is rawest, and the dense fog is densest, and the muddy streets are muddiest, near that leaden-headed old obstruction, appropriate ornament for the threshold of a leaden-headed old corporation: Temple Bar. And hard by Temple Bar, in Lincoln's Inn Hall, at the very heart of the fog, sits the Lord High Chancellor in his High Court of Chancery.

**Chancery was a type of court.*

ISBN 9780170244213

Using your annotations, answer the following questions in as much detail as possible.

1 Analyse how the writer sets his scene.

In your answer you should:

- Identify and give examples of **techniques** used in the text and explain their **effects**. (Techniques might include sentence structure, tense, vocabulary, allusion, simile, metaphor, personification, alliteration...)
- Show understanding of the **scene** the writer is revealing.
- Show understanding of the overall desired **impact** of the passage.

ISBN 9780170244213

2 Analyse how the writer achieves a focus for the reader.

In your answer you should:

- Identify and give examples of **techniques** used in the text and explain their effects. (e.g. repetition, sentence structure, adjectives, vocabulary, narrative style...)
- Show understanding of the development of **ideas** in the passage.
- Show understanding of the writer's **overall purpose**.

ISBN 9780170244213

On your own

We hope that this first section of ***Achievement English @ Year 12*** has reminded you that you know a great deal about how to read a text, how to analyse the writer's creative techniques and how to express your understanding.

Now it's time to put these skills into practice on your own.

First ...

Here is the full text of a short story. Do what you always do:

- Read it once to enjoy the tale and to see what happens.
- Read it again (and again) highlighting and/or underlining interesting techniques, effective vocabulary and structures, and looking up any words you might not fully understand.

  Clues:
  - similes,
  - onomatopoeia,
  - repetition,
  - personification,
  - effective verbs,
  - adverbs,
  - adjectives,
  - short and longer sentences,
  - sentence balance ...

- Then move on to the question after the text. Note exactly what you are being asked to write about.
- At this point you may well need to read parts of the text again, and more than once, as you seek the details to support your answers.

The Wasteland

The moment that the bus moved on he knew he was in danger, for by the lights of it he saw the figures of the young men waiting under the tree. That was the thing feared by all, to be waited for by young men. It was a thing he had talked about, now he was to see it for himself.

It was too late to run after the bus; it went down the dark street like an island of safety in a sea of perils. Though he had known of his danger only for a second, his mouth was already dry, his heart was pounding on his breast, something within him was crying out in protest against the coming event.

His wages were in his purse; he could feel them weighing heavily against his thigh. That was what they wanted from him. Nothing counted against that. His wife could be made a widow, his children made fatherless, nothing counted against that. Mercy was the unknown word.

ISBN 9780170244213

While he stood there irresolute he heard the young men walking towards him, not only from the side where he had seen them, but from the other also. They did not speak, their intention was unspeakable. The sound of their feet came on the wind to him. The place was well chosen, for behind him was the high wall of the convent, and the barred door that would not open before a man was dead. On the other side of the road was the waste land, full of wire and iron and the bodies of old cars. It was his only hope, and he moved towards it; as he did so he knew from the whistle that the young men were there too.

His fear was great and instant, and the smell of it went from his body to his nostrils. At that very moment one of them spoke, giving directions. So trapped was he that he was filled suddenly with strength and anger, and he ran towards the waste land swinging his heavy stick. In the darkness a form loomed up at him, and he swung the stick at it, and heard it give a cry of pain. Then he plunged blindly into the wilderness of wire and iron and the bodies of old cars.

Something caught him by the leg, and he brought his stick crashing down on it, but it was no man, only some knife-edged piece of iron. He was sobbing and out of breath, but he pushed on into the waste, while behind him they pushed on also, knocking against the old iron bodies and kicking against tins and buckets. He fell into some grotesque shape of wire; it was barbed and tore at his clothes and flesh. Then it held him, so that it seemed to him that death must be near, and having no other hope, he cried out, 'Help me, help me!' in which should have been a great voice but was voiceless and gasping. He tore at the wire, and it tore at him too, ripping his face and his hands.

Then suddenly he was free. He saw the bus returning, and he cried out again in the great voiceless voice, 'Help me, help me!' Against the lights of it he could plainly see the form of one of the young men. Death was near him, and for a moment he was filled with the injustice of life, that could end thus for one who had always been hard-working and law-abiding. He lifted the heavy stick and brought it down on the head of his pursuer, so that the man crumpled to the ground, moaning and groaning as though life had been unjust to him also.

Then he turned and began to run again, but ran first into the side of an old lorry which sent him reeling. He lay there for a moment expecting the blow that would end him, but even then his wits came back to him, and he turned over twice and

ISBN 9780170244213

was under the lorry. His very entrails seemed to be coming into his mouth, and his lips could taste sweat and blood. His heart was like a wild thing in his breast, and seemed to lift his whole body each time that it beat. He tried to calm it down, thinking it might be heard, and tried to control the noise of his gasping breath, but he could not do either of these things.

Then suddenly against the dark sky he saw two of the young men. He thought they must hear him; but they themselves were gasping like drowned men, and their speech came by fits and starts.

Then one of them said, 'Do you hear?'

They were silent except for their gasping, listening. And he listened also, but could hear nothing but his own exhausted heart.

'I heard a man ... running ... on the road,' said one.

'He's got away ... let's go.'

Then some more of the young men came up, gasping and cursing the man who had got away.

'Freddy,' said one, 'your father's got away.'

But there was no reply.

'Where's Freddie?' one asked.

One said, 'Quiet!' Then he called in a loud voice, 'Freddy.'

But still there was no reply.

'Let's go,' he said.

They moved off slowly and carefully, then one of them stopped.

'We are saved,' he said. 'Here is the man.'

He knelt down on the ground, and then fell to cursing.

'There's no money here,' he said.

One of them lit a match, and in the small light of it the man under the lorry saw him fall back.

'It's Freddy,' one said. 'He's dead.'

Then the one who had said, 'Quiet' spoke again.

ISBN 9780170244213

The man under the lorry heard them struggling with the body of the dead young man, and he turned once, twice, deeper into his hiding-place. The young men lifted the body and swung it under the lorry so that it touched him. Then he heard them moving away, not speaking, slowly and quietly, making an occasional sound again some obstruction in the waste.

He turned on his side, so that he would not need to touch the body of the young man. He buried his face in his arms, and said to himself in the idiom of his own language, 'People, arise! The world is dead.' Then he arose himself, and went heavily out of the waste land.

Alan Paton

Alan Paton was born in South Africa, worked as a teacher, the principal of a reformatory for black African youth and as a writer. You can find out more about him and his work on the Internet.

Now ...

We have given you a single question, but it has three parts. You might highlight the three parts in different colours and then, when you are composing your answer, use the same technique to check that you have actually answered all three parts of the question.

1 Which line is the turning-point in this story? What were you expecting before this and how did the writer create your expectation? Why is the ending of the story powerful?

ISBN 9780170244213

Where to now?

For simplicity's sake we have divided the types of text commonly used to assess your close reading skills into four different sections:

- prose
- poetry
- visual
- oral.

In this way you can practise your skills in the different areas you would more likely find certain types of language features. However do not think that you will only be asked about similes while analysing poetry or sentence structure with prose. Language features are from a universal group, and authors, whether they are journalists, poets, speech-writers or novelists, are expert at using all of them.

A simile is a simile is a simile. Whether it's for a poem or for an advert.

What's important is how and why it has been used.

ISBN 9780170244213

5 Text type 1: Prose

'Prose' means anything written that is not poetry. Prose passages for close reading may be classified under the headings: fact and fiction.

Fact	Fiction
Factual passages are from sources like: • Magazines • Newspapers • Non-fiction books • Advertising.	Fictional passages are from sources like: • Novels • Novellas • Short stories • Play scripts.

Remember though, there can be debate over what is fact and what is invented. A novel may be based on a writer's experience.

A magazine article purporting to be an 'interview' with a famous person may be largely invented. These days, separating fact from fiction on the Internet is a huge issue.

What will you be asked about?

When it comes to written prose passages you could be asked to look at a variety of different things:

- **ideas** (e.g. themes, attitudes, beliefs, experiences, feelings, insights, meanings, opinions, thoughts and understandings within the text)
- **language features** (e.g. word choice, syntax, sound devices)
- **structure** (e.g. part text, whole text, narrative, sequence beginnings and endings) as used for particular audiences and purposes
- **text conventions**.

Terminology you should be confident with …

In Year 12 it is important to include the technical language of English in your answer. The following list is what we would expect you to know at this level.

You will notice in the left hand margin there are two circles labelled 'I know' and 'I need to check'. Read through the list and tick the box that best describes your knowledge of each literary term. Look up all the ones you don't know in the Language Lists at the end of this book.

ISBN 9780170244213

I know	I need to check	
○	○	Abstract noun
○	○	Adjective
○	○	Adverb
○	○	Alliteration
○	○	Assonance
○	○	Cliché
○	○	Collective noun
○	○	Colloquial language
○	○	Common noun
○	○	Comparative adjective
○	○	Conjunction
○	○	Emotive language

I know	I need to check	
○	○	Extended metaphor
○	○	Hyperbole
○	○	Imagery
○	○	Jargon
○	○	Metaphor
○	○	Noun
○	○	Onomatopoeia
○	○	Parts of speech
○	○	Personification
○	○	Preposition
○	○	Pronoun
○	○	Pun

I know	I need to check	
○	○	Repetition
○	○	Rhetorical question
○	○	Sentence construction
○	○	Simile
○	○	Slang
○	○	Superlative
○	○	Verb

New to you may be …

Euphemism

A mild, indirect term for a blunt, direct or offensive phrase. For example: 'John's grandfather passed away' instead of 'John's grandfather died'. Some euphemisms may be less mild. Consider 'kicked the bucket' and 'popped his clogs'. A euphemism may create a humorous effect or offer insight into a character's personality. It may be intended to take the sting out of a negative comment.

Irony

The method of expression in which the ordinary meaning of the word is more or less the opposite of what the speaker/writer intends. For example: In *Pride and Prejudice* by Jane Austen, Mr Bennett stops his daughter Mary from playing any longer on the piano at a party by saying 'That will do extremely well, child. You have delighted us long enough.' It might seem like praise on the surface but is not; Mary plays poorly and is disconcerted by her father's words. The effect of irony draws attention to the real meaning behind the words and may convey a character or writer's attitude. Irony may also be used to create humour.

ISBN 9780170244213

Allusion

An indirect reference to a person or event. These may be, but are not necessarily, people and events in mythology and history.

For example: 'Sticky wicket' is a difficult situation demanding coolness and judgement. An allusion to the game of cricket.

'He's a shark' means a swindler, extortionist. An allusion to a shark, which snatches up its food, alive or dead.

'He's carrying the weight of the world on his shoulders' means he seems to be very worried. An allusion to the mythological figure of Atlas.

An allusion can create an added dimension to an image often by a comparison between similar qualities in the subject and in what is being alluded to.

Narrative voice

Narrative means telling of events.

Novels and short stories may be written in the third person (**he** walked along the road ... **she** ate a red apple ... **they** went to the movies together). The writer may present information about these characters by describing what they do or where they are. They may mix dialogue in with narrative to show what the characters think or feel. The writer may choose to show what just one character thinks and feels and leave the reader to make their own minds up about the other characters. The writer may choose to reveal everything about everyone. This is called the omniscient narrator or eye-of-god technique.

The writer may choose to write in the first person:

- **I** walked along the road.
- **I** saw **J**odie eating a red apple.
- **We** went to the movies together.

This 'I' is not the writer, it is the character invented by the writer. The writer may choose to have one character narrate (speak) the whole story:

- **I** was eating a red apple yesterday when, would you believe it, **I** met Antony, a really cool guy, in the street and out of the blue he said to **me** ...

Again, this is not the narrator, it is the character speaking and the language used by this narrator helps you to learn more about the character.

Occasionally writers use the second person (you). But this is usually not found in fictional writing.

Writers often use their own experience or feelings as a starting point, especially in poetry. It can be more difficult to decide whether it is the writer's own voice or that of a persona in a poem written in the first person. This is why it can be useful to know something about the life story of the poet when you read his or her poetry.

ISBN 9780170244213

Tense (from the Latin, meaning time)

The form of the verb that indicates the time of the action. There are three main tenses; past, present and future.

PAST	PAST CONTINUOUS	PRESENT	PRESENT CONTINUOUS	FUTURE	FUTURE CONTINUOUS
I brought I took I saw	I was bringing I was taking I was seeing	I bring I take I see	I am bringing I am taking I am seeing	I will bring I will take I will see	I will be bringing I will be taking I will be seeing

You should also be able to recognise the active and passive voice:

ACTIVE	PASSIVE
I took I saw Tom hit the ball.	I was taken I was seen The ball was hit by Tom.

Things get a lot more complicated than this!

Denotation/Connotation

Denotation is the dictionary meaning of a word. Connotation is the implied or suggested meaning. For example, the word 'mother' denotes one who has given birth. However the word 'mother' may have the connotation of female, caring, sensible, loving, practicality, experience, homemaker and so on.

Syntax

Syntax is a word derived from Greek, which means 'to put in order'. It is a branch of grammar dealing with:

a the arrangement of words in sentences

b the correct use of parts of speech

c the classification of sentences according to their clause structure.

As a speaker of English you already know how words are arranged to make sense. Consider these four words: *Sam, the, ball, hit*. By putting the words in different orders you can change their meaning:

Sam hit the ball.
The ball hit Sam.
'Hit the ball, Sam!'

You have been learning about parts of speech, too. You now understand that the function of a particular word in a sentence affects how we label it. For example:

The forestry worker used a *saw* (noun) to cut off the branches of the fallen tree.

I *saw* (verb) a yacht sail on the sea.

The *church* (adjective) spire was silhouetted against the sky.

The *church* (noun) stood in the centre of town.

ISBN 9780170244213

The language of prose

To sum up, this chart draws together all of the terminology you will use as you close read prose. Use it as a reference whenever you look at a piece of unfamiliar prose text.

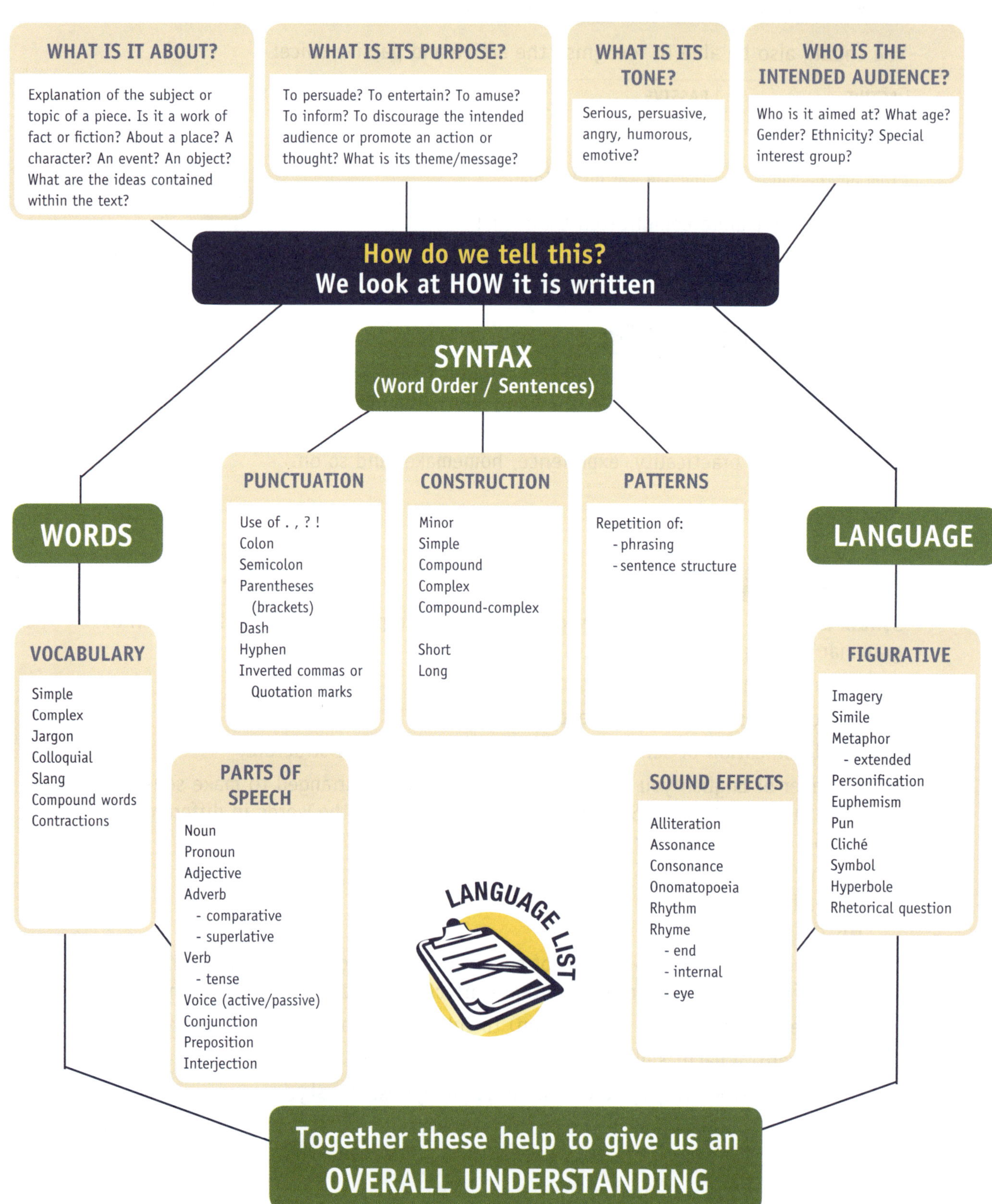

ISBN 9780170244213

Let's look at a writer's use of techniques

This is an extract from *The Two Towers*, Volume 2 of *The Lord of the Rings* by J.R.R. Tolkien. Read the passage. Annotate important features (see page 11 and/or 36).

The attack on Helm's Deep

It was now past midnight. The sky was utterly dark, and the stillness of the heavy air foreboded storm. Suddenly the clouds were seared by a blinding flash. Branched lightning smote down upon the eastward hills. For a staring moment the watchers on the walls saw all the space between them and the Dike lit with white light: it was boiling and crawling with black shapes, some squat and broad, some tall and grim, with high helms and sable shields. Hundreds and hundreds more were pouring over the Dike and through the breach. The dark tide flowed up to the walls from cliff to cliff. Thunder rolled in the valley. Rain came lashing down.

Arrows thick as the rain came whistling over the battlements, and fell clinking and glancing on the stones. Some found a mark. The assault on Helm's Deep had begun, but no sound or challenge was heard within; no answering arrows came.

The assailing hosts halted, foiled by the silent menace of rock and wall. Ever and again the lightning tore aside the darkness. Then the Orcs screamed, waving spear and sword, and shooting a cloud of arrows at any that stood revealed upon the battlements; and the men of the Mark amazed looked out, as it seemed to them, upon a great field of dark corn, tossed by a tempest of war, and every ear glinted with barbed light.

Brazen trumpets sounded. The enemy surged forward, some against the Deeping Wall, others towards the causeway and the ramp that led up to the Hornburg-gates. There the hugest Orcs were mustered, and the wild men of the Dunland fells. A moment they hesitated and then on they came. The lightning flashed, and blazoned upon every helm and shield the ghastly hand of Isengard was seen. They reached the summit of the rock; they drove towards the gates.

Then at last an answer came: a storm of arrows met them, and a hail of stones. They wavered, broke, and fled back; and then charged again, broke and charged again; and each time, like the incoming sea, they halted at a higher point. Again trumpets rang, and a press of roaring men leaped forth. They held their great shields above them like a roof, while in their midst they bore two trunks of mighty trees. Behind them orc-archers crowded, sending a hail of darts against the bowmen on the walls. They gained the gates. The trees, swung by strong arms, smote the timbers with a rending boom. If any man fell, crushed by a stone hurtling from above, two others sprang to take his place. Again and again the great rams swung and crashed.

Eomer and Aragorn stood together on Deeping Wall. They heard the roar of voices and the thudding of the rams; and then in a sudden flash of light they beheld the peril of the gates.

'Come!' said Aragorn. 'This is the hour when we draw swords together!'

ISBN 9780170244213

Answer the following questions in as much detail as possible:

1 General understanding

Explain in your own words what is happening in this passage.

2 Figures of speech

a The writer uses comparisons many times in this passage to enliven the description. Examples of both similes and metaphors have been underlined. Use colour highlighting to annotate which is which in the passage. Choose one of each and explain why you think the writer chose to use each one.

Simile

Explanation

Metaphor

Explanation

b The writer uses alliteration. Choose one example from paragraph 5 and comment on why the writer has used it.

Example

Explanation

3 Choice of vocabulary

a What figure of speech is being used in all these words? Explain their effect in the passage.

whistling, **clinking** (line 8), **boom** (line 27), **crashed** (line 28), **roar** (line 29), **thudding** (line 30)

Figure of speech

Effect

ISBN 9780170244213

b What part of speech are all these words? Are they well chosen? Why?

surged (line 16), **drove** (line 20), **charged** (line 22), **leaped** (line 24), **sprang** (line 27)

Part of speech ____________________

Reasons for choice ____________________

____

____

c What is the function of these words in paragraph 1? What do they add to the description?

utterly, **heavy**, **white**, **black**, **dark**

____

____

____

____

4 Syntax/Sentence structure

a There are **three** types of sentences in paragraph 2. Name each one.

i ____________________

ii ____________________

iii ____________________

b In paragraph 3 the writer uses two short sentences and then one long one. Why do you think he chooses to do this?

____

____

____

____

____

____

5 Response

Is this passage successful? Why/why not?

____

____

____

____

____

____

ISBN 9780170244213

Prose close reading practice

A variety of prose texts and accompanying questions are provided in this section to help you to practise your close reading.

Text 1

Read the following passage carefully. It is an article from a newspaper by a regular contributing writer. Annotate important features (see page 11 and/or 36).

Language police constantly looking to have the last word

One city newspaper has a couple of columnists who regularly attack the rampant illiteracy eroding New Zealand's educational and moral fibre.

You know the sort of thing. Inability to use its/it's, there/their, to/too correctly. Spelling that offers rhythm/rythmn/rythum. American abominations such as lite/thru/kleen.

The columnists round up the usual offenders: American television, video games, lazy parents, antediluvian and trendy-lefty teachers. They have not yet reached the imaginative heights of a spokesman for Pauline Hanson's One Nation party, who blamed it all on Asian immigrants.

Two things intrigue me about these condemnations. One is the intellectual flexibility which can call teachers both antediluvian and trendy lefties. The other is the blend of glee and moral zeal the writers show.

The glee is something we have all felt. Yes, it's shocking to read a menu listing 'vegetrain' dishes and 'deserts complimented by liqeurs.' But doesn't it make you feel smugly pleased that you know better?

The moral zeal seems marginally ludicrous. I agree that an inability to distinguish between comprise/compose, uninterested/disinterested, replace/substitute heralds the imminent collapse of society. But can't we live with it?

The trouble is, of course, that it's change. And all columnists feel threatened by change – unless they are under 30, when they fret that things are not changing enough.

Historical linguistics show that language is always altering, just like fashion, art and culture. Grammar and spelling are essentially protean and fluid.

Attempts to prevent language change are lost causes. The Italians tried to legislate against such evolution. The French also imposed language-freezing rules. Both failed. (Can you imagine anything French doing what it's told? Look at their rugby backline.)

ISBN 9780170244213

Okay, it's dreadful to see someone write 'Aprylle showres' – except that is how Chaucer did spell it. And what brought us from Chaucer to our present spelling? Fashion, pronunciation, trial and error, personal preferences, ignorance.

Yes, the same factors that operate now. Presumably 14th to 19th century columnists also fulminated against them.

I know rules are about preventing chaos. They are also about power, so they are usually imposed by those over a certain age.

You cannot help noticing that the grammar and spelling to which these columnists and others object are usually that of the young. The illiterate, deprived, antediluvian, trendy, teacher-suffering young.

Here's a scary thought. Black English vernacular (BEV), the English spoken by American blacks, is now recognised as a distinct language. What if youth culture claims its own, officially separate language? They could call it Young Users Patois (YUP), and nobody could legitimately attack its spelling and syntax.

Disturbingly, some of the spelling that so offends older guardians is a more accurate rendering of current pronunciation than conventional forms. Think of 'envirment'. Or 'govmernt', which carries the bonus of that evocative second-syllable slur.

Experiments and errors help to move language. Some of them are disastrous. Some are fortuitous. I enjoy the lurch of perspective that comes from realising 'assizes' means Aussies. And how marvellous to have it confirmed that most transtasman types should be up before a judge.

Condemnation of spelling and grammar lapses is often an aesthetic judgment – and, therefore, a subjective one. My taste good, your taste bad.

I also hate 'lite' and 'nite', and I shudder in anticipation of 'nitelite'. I wince when Wanda the air hostess says we are stopping outside of the terminal and some people are continuing on to Wellington.

I wince at her redundancy and her rhythms. After all, they are different rhythms from mine. I also snarl at the clunkiness of 'real windy', but I know that others like its snap and speed.

Other ages, other tastes. All part of the incessant interplay between tradition and experiment.

I am not saying that near enough is good enough but that mutations sometimes advance a species. And that out of a lot of silly mistakes and posturing, great results may come. A bit of colour, as opposed to the black and white (and grey) of rules.

Can't we chuckle as well as chafe at reading that someone has deported this life? Especially if he is one of those assizes.

Similarly, I envy a friend whose restaurant bill ('non-vegetrain') told him he had been 'serviced by Rayleen'.

And who can possibly condemn apparent illiteracy when it means you are told that the Pauline Hanson spokesman of my opening paragraphs actually came from the One Notion party?

As one of my wife's seventh formers wrote, I reset my case.

by David Hill, a Taranaki writer

ISBN 9780170244213

Before you go further …

Complete the following chart.

What is it **about**?	What is the **purpose**?	What is the **tone**?	Who is the **audience**?

Answer the following questions in as much detail as possible:

1 How can you tell that this is a personal opinion?

2 Describe the tone of the passage (think tone of voice). How is it conveyed?

3 Give two examples of spelling errors noted in the passage. Correct the errors.

i

ii

4 Give one example of a grammatical error noted in the passage.

5 Give two examples of the way a humorous effect is created in the article.

i

ii

6 'My taste good, your taste bad' is an allusion. To what? Explain what it means.

ISBN 9780170244213

7 What is the reason for the use of parentheses in paragraph 9?

8 Give two examples of acronyms from the passage and explain what they mean.

i

ii

9 Give an example of a neologism in the passage.

10 In your own words explain the central reasons for having language rules, according to the writer.

11 Summarise in your own words the attitude of the writer toward changes in language use and provide quotations to support your opinion.

An aside on ... neologisms

A neologism is a newly coined term, word or phrase, that may be in the process of entering common use, but has not yet been accepted into mainstream language. A neologism may be a completely new word, for instance the word 'astronaut' meaning space traveller was coined in the 20th century. Or an existing word can be given a new meaning: 'mouse' for a device to control a computer.

Text 2

Read the following passage carefully. It is an article from a newspaper by a regular contributing writer. Annotate important features (see page 11 and/or 36).

Correct language deserves more than just lip service

Accepting that language is constantly changing is no excuse for being casual about the teaching of grammar and spelling, writes C.K. Stead.

David Hill's Dialogue article on our changing language is a typical example of Mr Facing Both Ways.

On the one hand, he wouldn't be found dead with an ungrammatical sentence, in his head or on his page, spells impeccably, and knows all the right linguistic distinctions and the traps to be avoided. On the other hand he wants to show that he's a democrat, one of the lads, up with the play, modern.

Hill's argument is based on a false either/or. Either you believe in a hard and fast set of language rules, or anything goes.

Since it's easy to show (and he's right in this) that language is constantly changing and over time will break out of any set of rules you make for it, the logical conclusion seems to be that anything goes, and that those who insist that one usage is "correct" and another "incorrect" are silly old stick-in-the-muds fighting a battle they can't win.

My most recent book, The Writer at Work, contains an essay called "English in our schools," which deals at some length with schoolteachers who promote this kind of argument. It is used as an excuse for teaching no grammar, being casual about spelling (including their own), and treating any attempt to improve children's written or spoken language as a cruel attack on their sense of confidence.

There is a middle point between rigidity and chaos, and that is what ought to be aimed for. To take an example Hill offers: usage is changing, so "disinterested" which once meant "objective," is being used so often to mean "uninterested" it seems certain that that will soon be its predominant, or even its only, meaning.

I agree there's no point in attempting to stop the process – though there is no need, either, to hurry it along. However, a good teacher will teach this as an example of a shift in usage, perhaps also remarking that an educated person knows that the change is happening, watches it happen, and makes a conscious choice to use the word in one of its two senses, while an uneducated person manifests the change in ignorance.

On the whole, given the choice, most people prefer knowledge to ignorance. Hill seems to be promoting ignorance – for others, of course, not for himself.

Teaching grammar, spelling and pronunciation according to an agreed set of current conventions is a way of aiding good order and easy communication. It is not the same as asking that those conventions be set in concrete.

Nor is it damaging children. On the contrary, it is helping them to point out that certain uses of language will signal to those who have power in our society – and even to the nice Mr Facing Both Ways, who reserves the right to have a good chuckle at those who make mistakes – that the speaker or writer is an educated person; and that other uses will signal an ill-educated or uneducated person.

This is a fact of our society, and it is surely part of the work of teaching English to make it known.

On the subject of spelling, Hill gives the example of "Aprylle showres," which, he tells us, is how Chaucer spelled it. He suggests some of the elements – fashion, trial and error, personal preference and so on – that brought about the change over centuries, and points out that the same forces are at work in the present. "Presumably," he goes on, "14th to 19th century columnists fulminated against them."

There were, of course, no 14th century columnists because there were no newspapers. And no one in the 14th century would have complained of any of the three spellings of that phrase I can find in editions of Chaucer on my shelves, because English spelling was not standardised until the early 18th century.

It was standardised for convenience because it made pages of printed text more immediately and unambiguously meaningful, which Hill believes others – young folk, not himself – should feel free to abandon.

As for his advice that rather than complain about the decline in standards of written and spoken language, we should laugh at the howlers it brings about: well, of course, one does laugh. But it seems strange to present yourself as a liberal, humane defender of "the young, the illiterate, the deprived," and then suggest the mistakes we give them licence to make will provide us with first-class entertainment.

■ C.K.Stead is a novelist, poet and Emeritus Professor of English at the University of Auckland.

It is always interesting to read the other side of an argument. C.K. Stead thinks differently from David Hill. Reread Hill's ideas on pages 40–41. With whom do you agree?

ISBN 9780170244213

Before you go further ...

Complete the following chart.

What is it **about**?	Who is the **audience**?	What is the **style**?	What is the **purpose**?

Answer the following questions in as much detail as possible:

1 What reasons does C.K. Stead give for teaching correct grammar?

2 How does he attack the previous writer and his opinions?

3 What is your opinion? Do you want to learn the conventions of grammar, spelling, punctuation and pronunciation?

ISBN 9780170244213

Text 3

Read the following passage carefully. Annotate important features (see page 11 and/or 36).

Schools are getting low marks for environmental awareness in their daily maintenance.

Sustainability is a key issue for organisations internationally and the number one global issue for the contract cleaning industry.

It's also a major focus for schools. The New Zealand Curriculum emphasises that children should learn about sustainability and environmental responsibility and the Enviroschools website reveals that over 730 schools are involved in sustainability initiatives.

However, when it comes to sustainable approaches to cleaning, many schools are at the bottom of the class compared to other public sector organisations.

School boards are, understandably, primarily focused on costs and budgets and under pressure to put as much money as possible into the delivery of education.

Few board members will be experienced in technical matters around cleaning and their instinct may be to go for the cheapest option, with little consideration of the impact that may have on the fabric of their school and the wider environment.

If a building is not being cleaned using the most appropriate products and methods, then it will deteriorate. Savings made on cleaning will, ultimately, come back to bite in increased capital costs.

New Zealand's cleaning industry has made huge strides towards more socially and environmentally sustainable cleaning methods.

The introduction of innovative microfibre products, which clean surfaces without scratching, reduce bacteria and prevent cross contamination far more effectively than conventional cleaning methods, have been of huge benefit.

Alternatives to chemical cleaners have been developed and automatic dosing systems introduced to ensure that products are used as efficiently as possible.

Many cleaning companies have moved from a one size fits all approach to recognising the importance of the relationship between the client, the cleaner and the supplier.

Is your school board working with your cleaner to ensure that their staff are well trained and using the most suitable and sustainable products? The chemicals used for the factory along the road may not be the most appropriate for your environment.

Nowadays most cleaning companies carry a range of different products, often including both chemical and non chemical options, and select the best for each contract based on experience and consultation with the supplier and client.

Approaches to waste have changed dramatically. While our BSCNZ members used to be responsible for removing and disposing of waste from a site, now many work with clients to find solutions involving partial or total recycling and which might even be cost neutral.

Achieving sustainable cleaning in the face of budget restraints is achievable.

The New Zealand health sector, for example, has been remarkably open to change. Despite being under extreme pressure in terms of cost cutting, DHBs continue to explore new sustainable opportunities.

Schools have a head start. Most are already cleaned during daylight hours, something New Zealand businesses are increasingly adopting as socially sustainable, enabling cleaners to work family-friendly hours, and significantly reducing energy consumption.

I believe that schools have an incredible opportunity to be leaders in the drive towards sustainable cleaning, but this requires a change in focus within school boards and leadership from principals.

New Zealand organisations with successful sustainable cleaning and waste policies have recognised that commitment to change needs to come from the very top and be driven through every facet of the business.

You need to change your culture and bring everybody onside. Ninety-nine percent of your staff might be recycling waste paper, but the integrity of the paper will be destroyed by a few apple cores being thrown into recycling bins.

New Zealand schools are nurturing the young people who will ultimately work for or lead these organisations. Isn't this the most fantastic opportunity to prepare them to do so in the most sustainable ways?

Ultimately change will come, as school boards recognise that, in the long term, sustainable approaches to cleaning are the most economical. But why wait?

Brian Young

ISBN 9780170244213

Before you go further ...

Complete the following chart.

What is it **about?**	Who is the **audience?**	What is the **style?**	What is the **purpose?**

Answer the following questions in as much detail as possible:

1 How does the writer indicate that sustainability is an important issue?

2 How and why does the writer use metaphor? Choose two metaphors for your answer.

3 What are the problems for schools with achieving sustainability?

4 What three recent developments are improving cleaning practices?

5 How does the writer promote recycling?

6 Why is daylight cleaning a good idea?

7 How does the writer illustrate the reason why everyone needs to support recycling?

8 At whom is this article aimed. How can you tell?

ISBN 9780170244213

9 Examine the technique used to persuade the reader in the final two paragraphs.

10 Based on what you have read, what is your opinion of your school's cleaning and recycling methods?

Text 4

Read the following passage carefully. It is from the beginning of a short story *Madeline* written by Shonagh Koea. Annotate important features (see page 11 and/or 36).

The main thing about it was, as Teddy O'Reilly's mother said later, that it brought them all together. The whole episode was an example of the inherent solidarity of the entire district. As for Kevin – known as Kev-Boy since he went to kindergarten and there were two Kevs in the tiny-tots class – the way he took it was nothing short of abso-bloody-lutely marvellous, as they all said.

A great guy, a fabulous sportsman, an out-of-this-world bloke and a real catch for any girl. That is what they all said, and he got quite a few rounds shouted afterwards, in succeeding days, just so he could see they were all right behind him abso-bloody-lutely one hundred per cent at the Old Cal – which is what they usually called the Caledonian Hotel, scene of the debacle. One or two of them, maybe even half a dozen or a dozen, even fifty, had a quick word with him about what sort of girl he really needed and claimed that it was just that, up till the time of the after-match party, he had somehow mistakenly made it his habit to hang out with flash sheilas which was a big mistake in the nature of an otherwise really great bloke.

'And flash sheilas,' said Bert Burtt, the local retired fencing contractor, 'are just bad news, Kev-Boy my son,' as he clapped him on a brawny shoulder. They all hoped in their various ways – some behind closed doors and others more vociferously

ISBN 9780170244213

in the pie shop or the Old Cal – that he had now given up this type of person. The truly awful evening they had had to spend with Madeline might, they hoped, have taught him a real lesson. At least two dozen people said that Madeline, single-handedly, had almost ruined the party after the Littledene Rugby Subunion final by simply not fitting into the social mores that usually pertained at such gatherings. Five people, as yet un-named, claimed to have heard her say several times that she wanted to go home and where could she ring for a taxi? Someone else said she refused to hang her coat on the coathooks in the ladies' cloakroom and asked if there were coat-hangers, preferably padded.

Kev-Boy's mother let it be known later that she had told him in no uncertain terms she wanted a nice plain girl brought home, a local girl please and nothing flashy from the city, thank you laddie, and preferably with good, strong, big legs so she could work around the place if need be.

'I came right out in the open with it,' she said at sewing circle the following week, 'and told him straight what I thought.'

'And so you should.' A dozen kind and caring hands darted forward, sewing or knitting discarded, to pat her shoulder. Mavis Teasdale, who was Tony Jones's wife's brother's sister-in-law's auntie by marriage, went and put the kettle on, her feet echoing on the bare boards of the church hall. Support, she thought, was what was needed.

'I think we'll have our cuppa early,' she said for no apparant reason and the others, as they all said on the telephone to each other later, tactfully remained silent so Kev-Boy's mother would not notice their concern.

'Townies.' That was Granny Trump. 'Who wants them? I told Alan my grandson,' she said in a determinedly quavering voice, 'when he started playing at first five-eighth that if he brought home a girl from the city I'd stop making damson jam. A girl from the city – and with thin legs too – is not what a good first five-eighth wants. I told him.'

Before you go further …

Complete the following chart.

What is it **about**?	Who is the **audience**?	What is the **style**?	What is the **purpose**?

ISBN 9780170244213

Answer the following questions in as much detail as possible:

1 Colloquial language is used several times in this extract. Give **three** examples and explain why the writer has chosen to use colloquial language in the story.

i ______________________ ii ______________________ iii ______________________

2 The writer draws largely on reported speech in this short story. Give **one** example of reported and **one** example of direct speech.

Reported speech ______________________

Direct speech ______________________

3 The extract shows how news is passed on and reframed in the local community. Where do the people talk?

4 How do you know this story is set in a rural area?

5 The opening sentence talks about the 'inherent solidarity of the district'. What does this mean and how is it revealed?

6 What does the word 'vociferously' (para 3) mean?

ISBN 9780170244213

7 In paragraph 1 the hyphen is used in three different ways. Identify and explain each.

i

ii

iii

8 Madeline, we are told, nearly spoilt the party 'by simply not fitting into the social mores that usually pertained at such gatherings'. How does the writer illustrate this 'not fitting in'?

9 What is the attitude of the writer to Madeline? Explain her attitude and say how it is conveyed in the story.

10 Explain your opinion of this community based on what the writer has told you and the tone of the passage. Make at least three references to the text.

ISBN 9780170244213

Text 5

Read the following passage carefully. It is from a newspaper columnist. Dave Barry is well-known for his humorous writings about life. Annotate important features (see page 11 and/or 36).

Scary kids

Dave Barry

TODAY'S scary topic for parents is: What Your Children Do When You're Not Home.

I have a letter from New York working mum Judy Price concerning her 14-year-old son David, "who should certainly know better, because the school keeps telling me he is a genius, but I have not seen signs of this in our normal, everyday life."

Judy states that one day when she came home from work, David met her outside and said: "Hi, Mum. Are you going in?"

(This is a bad sign, parents.) Judy says she considered replying, "No, I thought I'd just stay here in the car all night and pull away for work in the morning."

That actually would have been a wise idea. Instead, she went inside, where she found a large black circle burned into the middle of her kitchen counter.

"DAVID," she screamed. "WHAT WERE YOU COOKING?"

The soft, timid reply came back: "A baseball," Judy writes. "Of course. What else could it be? How could I forget to tell my children never to cook a baseball? It's my fault, really.

It turns out that according to David's best friend's cousin — and if you can't believe HIM, who CAN you believe? — you can hit a baseball three times as far if you really heat it up first.

So David did this, and naturally he put the red-hot pan down directly onto the counter top, probably because there was no rare antique furniture available.

For the record: David claims that the heated baseball did, in fact, go farther. But this does NOT mean that you young readers should try this dangerous and foolish experiment at home. Use a friend's home.

No, seriously, you young people should never heat up a baseball without proper adult supervision, just as you should never — and I say this from personal experience — attempt to make a rumba box.

A rumba box is an obscure musical instrument that consists of a wooden box with metal strips attached to it in such a way that when you plunk them, the box resonates with a pleasant rhythmic sound.

The only time I ever saw a rumba box was in 1964, when a friend of my parents, named Walter Karl, played at a gathering at our house, and it sounded great.

Mr Karl said the metal strips were actually pieces of the spring from an old-fashioned wind-up phonograph. This gave my best friend, Lanny Watts, an idea. He realised two things:

1. His parents had an old-fashioned wind-up gramophone they hardly ever used.

2. They both worked out of the home.

So Lanny and I decided to make our own rumba box. Our plan, as I recall it, was to take the phonograph apart, snip off a bit of the spring, then put the gramophone back together, and nobody would be the wiser. This plan worked perfectly until we removed the metal box that held the gramophone spring: this box turned out to be very hard to open.

"Why would they make it so strong?" we asked ourselves.

Finally, recalling the lessons we had learned about mechanical advantage in high school physics class, we decided to hit the box with a sledge-hammer.

Do you remember the climactic scene in the movie Raiders of the Lost Ark, when the nazis open up the Ark of the Covenant, and out surges a terrifying horde of evil fury and the nazis' heads melt like chocolate bunnies in a microwave? Well, that's similar to what happened when Lanny sledge-hammered the spring box.

It turns out that the reason the box is so strong is that there is a really powerful, tightly wound, extremely irritable spring in there, and when you let it out, it just goes berserk, writhing and snarling and thrashing violently all over the room, seeking revenge on all the people who have cranked it over the years.

Lanny and I fled the room until the spring calmed down. When we returned, we found phonograph parts spread all over the room, mixed in with about 3.8km of spring. We realised we'd have to modify our Project Goal slightly, from making a rumba box to being in an entirely new continent when Lanny's mother got home.

– KRT

ISBN 9780170244213

Before you go further ...

Complete the following chart.

What is it **about**?	Who is the **audience**?	What is the **style**?	What is the **purpose**?

Answer the following questions in as much detail as possible:

1 Explain the writer's choice of vocabulary and sentence structure in the title and opening paragraph. How are they linked? How can you tell this will be a humorous piece?

2 Paragraph 2 contains words in inverted commas. Why? What do these words add to the introduction?

3 What is the purpose of the brackets in paragraph 4?

4 Why are capital letters used in paragraph 6 and paragraph 8?

5 Explain why the writer refers to high school physics (column 3).

ISBN 9780170244213

6 Identify and comment on the extended metaphor used in the last two paragraphs.

7 The writer gives many examples of the way he believes 14-year-olds think. Make a general statement about his attitude and give at least **two** examples from the text to support your idea.

8 The writer uses hyperbole (exaggeration) and irony (saying the opposite of what is true) to create humour throughout this passage. Choose **three** examples of either exaggeration or irony and explain why each one is humorous.

i

ii

iii

9 Who is the intended audience of this piece?

ISBN 9780170244213

Text 6

Read the following carefully. It is an extract from *To the Lighthouse* by Virginia Woolf. Annotate important features (see page 11 and/or 36).

To the Lighthouse

... but then what was the point, she asked herself, of buying good chairs to let them spoil up here all through the winter when the house, with only one old woman to see to it, positively dripped with wet? Never mind: the rent was precisely twopence halfpenny; the children loved it; it did her husband good to be three thousand, or if she must be accurate, three hundred miles from his library and his lectures and his disciples; and there was room for visitors. Mats, camp beds, crazy ghosts of chairs and tables whose London life of service was done – they did well enough here; and a photograph or two, and books. Books, she thought, grew of themselves. She never had time to read them. Alas! even the books that had been given to her, and inscribed by the hand of the poet himself: 'For her whose wishes must be obeyed' ... 'The happier Helen of our days' ... disgraceful to say, she had never read them. And Croom on the Mind and Bates on the Savage Customs of Polynesia ('My dear, stand still,' she said) – neither of those could one send to the Lighthouse. At a certain moment, she supposed, the house would become so shabby that something must be done. If they could be taught to wipe their feet and not bring the beach in with them – that would be something. Crabs, she had to allow, if Andrew really wished to dissect them, or if Jasper believed that one could make soup from seaweed, one could not prevent it; or Rose's objects – shells, reeds, stones; for they were gifted, her children, but all in quite different ways. And the result of it was, she sighed, taking in the whole room from floor to ceiling, as she held the stocking against James's leg, that things got shabbier and shabbier summer after summer. The mat was fading; the wall-paper was flapping. You couldn't tell any more that those were roses on it. Still, if every door in a house is left perpetually open, and no lockmaker in the whole of Scotland can mend a bolt, things must spoil. What was the use of flinging a green Cashmere shawl over the edge of a picture frame? In two weeks it would be the colour of pea soup. But it was the doors that annoyed her; every door was left open. She listened. The drawing-room door was open; the hall door was open; it sounded as if the bedroom doors were open; and certainly the window on the landing was open, for that she had opened herself. That windows should be open, and doors shut – simple as it was, could none of them remember it?

Before you go further …

Complete the following chart.

What is it **about**?	Who is the **audience**?	What is the **style**?	What is the **purpose**?

Answer the following questions in as much detail as possible:

1 What facts do you learn about the woman from this passage?

2 Describe the house and how it is treated by its owners.

3 What is the woman's attitude towards reading? How do you know?

4 What is her attitude towards her children? Give at least **two** quotations to support your ideas.

5 Comment on the use of paragraphs.

ISBN 9780170244213

6 Identify the structure of sentence 2 and its purpose.

7 Give **two** examples of rhetorical questions used in the passage. Why are they there?

i

ii

Reason

8 Ellipsis marks are used in sentence 5. Why?

9 What is the woman doing while thinking these thoughts?

10 Explain in your own words the character that is being created in this passage. What is your opinion of the author's success in creating her? Support your answer with reference to the text.

ISBN 9780170244213

Text 7

Read the following passage carefully. It is an extract from the novel *The Godwits Fly* by Robin Hyde. Annotate important features (see page 11 and/or 36).

The pool was brown and stagnant, the irises around it still tightly furled, their purple hard in spikes; but the feel of the roughened turf, delicately harsh, and the streaks of green and yellow in patterns of osier leaves were ease enough. They drew aside into the ways of the trees. Long ago, someone had kept bees, and the white hives stood there, half decaying but full of their people, black bodies and thin wings clotted against combs oozing dark gold honey. The bees had taken to the tree tops for a living, bringing home the essence of manuka and rata, native honeys mixed with the sweet they sucked from the veins of cold pink belladonna lilies, <u>standing in surprised colonies on the edge of the pool</u>. When Eliza saw them she could only say, 'Wild pink lilies,' and draw her hand across her eyes, as if she half wanted to shut out the sight of them. And she did, for there is something dangerous in such perfection, and the cold statelihood of nature's things, reverted to their types, seemed to be best left alone. But she had no more than a moment to think of anything, for the sun beams shot <u>blanching</u> through the boughs, riding like cock-horses of supplejack and lancewood, and Timothy's eyes had the gilt prickles in them as he pulled her down, murmuring, 'Sit there. The light comes through the branches.' He picked up her hair and smothered it over her face, one strand after another ...

ISBN 9780170244213

Before you go further ...

Complete the following chart.

What is it **about**?	Who is the **audience**?	What is the **style**?	What is the **purpose**?

Answer the following questions in as much detail as possible:

1 Explain, in your own words, what is meant by '... their purple hard in spikes' (line 2).

2 Comment on the atmosphere of the sentence 'Long ago, someone had ... oozing dark gold honey.' (lines 4–7) and how it is created.

3 Identify the underlined poetic technique used in line 10 and explain the effect of the technique.

4 What is meant by the word 'blanching' (line 16)? Comment on the effect that it creates.

5 Quote and comment on how language is used to suggest the character of **either** Eliza **or** Timothy.

ISBN 9780170244213

Something a little different - SATIRE

What is satire?

Satire is a literary genre where individuals, certain groups of people or society itself are criticised. The vices or shortcomings, bad behaviour or foolishnesses of people are displayed and ridiculed in a way that is usually meant to be funny or humorous but often carries a serious meaning beneath the humour. Satirists seek change; want improvements in the world, therefore their writing can be seen as constructive criticism – especially by those who agree with them.

What techniques do satirists use?

A lot of irony. Irony is a literary technique that says the opposite of what it means. When used for satire, irony pretends to accept, even approve of, what the writer wishes to criticise or attack.

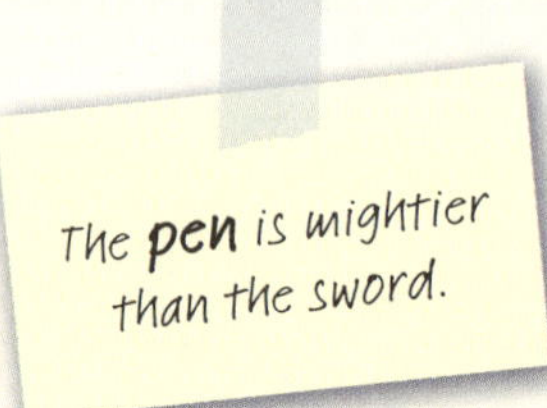

Well-known light-hearted irony currently in New Zealand is shown in these billboard messages. They are designed to be amusing/funny. They say the opposite of what they mean, followed by 'Yeah right' that highlights the irony! But they are also making a comment on something in our society.

When you read a piece of satire look for these techniques:

- Allusion
- Analogy
- Comparison
- Double entendre
- Hyperbole
- Irony
- Juxtaposition
- Parody

ISBN 9780170244213

Allusion

An indirect reference to an event or person. The effect is to extend an image or idea in the listener's mind.

Analogy

A similarity between two things that are otherwise different. All metaphors and similes are based on analogy.

Comparison

Similarities and/or differences between two people, places, ideas, or things are examined.

Double entendre

From the French meaning *double meaning.*

A word or phrase that can be interpreted in two ways, especially where one meaning is indelicate.

This type of humour depends on ambiguity. Ambiguity means unclear, imprecise meaning.

Hyperbole

Deliberate exaggeration.

Irony

The use of words that, when taken in context, are revealed to mean the opposite of what is said.

Juxtaposition

Words or phrases are placed side-by-side, especially for comparison or contrast, inviting the reader to make the connection and discover a meaning.

Parody

A humorous imitation of another piece of writing or performance. The parody is designed to ridicule the attitudes, style or subject matter of the original.

ISBN 9780170244213

This is a newspaper article written by a humorous columnist commenting on international politics. Mandelson, Blair and Alexander are British politicians. Gaddafi is the Libyan leader. Read the passage carefully. Annotate important features (see page 11 and/or 36).

I know, let's sell weapons to a lunatic

Only a few weeks ago Gaddafi was the West's eccentric friend, writes Mark Steel.

The Western leaders now condemning Colonel Muammar Gaddafi as a madman must be perplexed as to what's gone wrong with him, because up until a month ago they obviously thought he was perfectly sane and well-balanced — otherwise they wouldn't have sold him all those tanks. They must wonder if the stress of being a dictator has got to him, and if he'd had a fortnight off and started yoga all this trouble could have been avoided.

So maybe the best way to intervene is to send him to a good shrink. Then they could make a report for the United Nations that went: "His desire to refer to his fellow Libyans as 'Cockroaches' who must be killed suggest the patient is experiencing the trauma of feeling he's a woman trapped in a Colonel's body. And the need to make speeches while under an umbrella is a classic symptom of Obsessive Compulsive Disorder, so maybe we shouldn't send him any more tanks for at least three weeks, until he's better."

They should have been prepared for this, because they all said he was mad for thirty years, then suddenly decided he was rational about 10 years ago, by coincidence around the time he announced he'd back the West in the war on terror. To be fair, some of those who embraced him at this time are impressively unrepentant. For example, former British Labour politician Peter Mandelson insists when Gaddafi renounced his desire for weapons of mass destruction we had to "bring him into the fold" with deals for oil and arms.

Because when a dictator tells you he no longer wants destructive weapons, what else can you do but welcome his change of heart, by selling him a desertful of destructive weapons? It's like wandering up to someone at Alcoholics Anonymous and saying: "Congratulations on finally renouncing drink. Now let's go and get pissed."

Former British Prime Minister Tony Blair told us in 2007 "the commercial relationship between Britain and Libya is going from strength to strength". So everything was ideal, we could let a dictator sell us oil and buy our arms because he'd backed our war against a dictator, who used to sell us oil and buy our arms. If Saddam had said in 2001 he was willing to back our war against Gaddafi we'd have got so confused we'd have declared war on ourselves.

The people who defend the befriending of Gaddafi, such as Douglas Alexander, Britain's shadow foreign secretary, insist he promised he wouldn't use weapons such as tear gas "against his own people", which seems a liberal attitude towards someone you've derided as a madman for 30 years. Presumably Blair said to him: "Now I'm trusting you here, so if you DO open fire on thousands of protestors demanding a minimum wage, you'll not just be letting me down, you'll be letting yourself down."

In any case, who did we imagine Gaddafi might use this tear gas against? Perhaps he said: "Ah, Mr Blair, I fear at any moment we might be invaded by a nation of badgers."

So now we expect the rebels to be grateful if we offer them our services, because when Britain wants to help by sending an army into an Arab country what could possibly go wrong? It's like the builder who burned your house down ringing to say: "I hear you need your house rebuilt. We can offer very reasonable rates."

So the rebels seem to be aware that while the West can offer expert advice on the weaponry they're up against, seeing as it was the West that made it, on the other hand being supported by the British and American army won't help their aim of winning mass popularity among the Libyan people.

Because British and American leaders spent weekends with Gaddafi and arranged trade deals and hugged him for the press, and yet at no time did anyone spot he was in any way the sort of character you shouldn't send weapons to. And, in fact, even if he'd announced he had a split personality and then started talking in a high pitched voice insisting he was Sandra from Wolverhampton, Blair would have thought: "This is excellent news. We can sell tanks to both of them."

ISBN 9780170244213

Answer the following questions in as much detail as possible:

1 How does the opening paragraph suggest to the reader that this is a humorous piece?

2 What does the writer criticise about the West's dealings with Gaddafi?

3 How does the writer parody the language of psychology/psychiatry in this passage?

4 Choose **two** of these sentences and explain the technique/s used in each one:

   a Because when a dictator tells you he no longer wants destructive weapons, what else can you do but welcome his change of heart, by selling him a desertful of destructive weapons?

   b Presumably Blair said to him: 'Now I'm trusting you here, so if you DO open fire on thousands of protestors demanding a minimum wage, you'll not just be letting me down, you'll be letting yourself down.'

   c So now we expect the rebels to be grateful if we offer them our services, because when Britain wants to help by sending an army into an Arab country what could possibly go wrong?

5 What is the writer's intention by writing this column?

ISBN 9780170244213

Text type 2: Poetry

'Urgh' 'Not poetry' 'Do we have to?' 'I don't understand it.'

These are a selection of typical senior student responses when the word 'poetry' is mentioned.

But, if you think about it, everyone likes poetry. You will remember snippets of poems and songs all your life. For example:

- Hairy Maclary from Donaldson's Dairy
- Mary had a little lamb
- Up, up and away in my beautiful balloon.

We all enjoy rhythm, from the heartbeat as we grew within our mother's womb, to the clapping, counting, naming songs we learnt at kindy, 'ma is white, whero is red ...' to the songs we sang in the junior classes, 'run rabbit, run rabbit, run, run, run ...' to the pop music we enjoy(ed) as teenagers.

And we all like sounds:

- Onomatopoeia in 'pop goes the weasel'
- Alliteration in 'she sells sea shells by the sea shore'
- Rhyme in 'incy wincy spider'
- Repetition in 'who stole the cookie from the cookie jar?'

Think of rhymes, rhythms and sounds of words you personally enjoy and remember easily. Think nursery rhymes, songs, jingles, proverbs, sayings, quotations ...
List at least five of them here:

So when did it get so hard to enjoy and understand poetry?

Here is some simple advice ...

ISBN 9780170244213

How to approach a poem

1 **Don't worry.** A poem is not a puzzle that must be deciphered completely before you get the 'right' answer.

A poet spends a lot of time choosing exactly the best words for their poem. You may not understand them all or be able to see why they were chosen. That doesn't mean you cannot understand the idea that the poet is trying to share. Some poems you may be asked to read are written by and for people who have a lot more experience of life than you do at the moment. You can enjoy and understand parts of a poem without fully grasping it all.

2 When you study an unfamiliar text in class you may be given the text on a single sheet for annotation. If not, **make one for yourself** and add your own annotations.

3 Always **read a poem lots of times.** Try to read it aloud. The first poetry was meant to be spoken, or read aloud, just like children's poems and stories.

Make sure you read to the punctuation. Often an idea is not contained in each separate line.

4 **Decide what you think the poem is generally about.** There may be a simple surface meaning and a deeper one, too. Do this before you begin to look at the way the poet has chosen words and images, has used figures of speech and layout, to deliver that meaning. Sometimes the title can hint at the theme of a poem.

5 **Look at the poem in more detail.** Always ask yourself why the poet chose those particular words. Often you will be asked questions that guide you towards particular things like figures of speech (simile, metaphor, sound devices), parts of speech (nouns, verbs) and pattern (rhythm, rhyme, sentence structure). At this level it is important that you are able to recognise and name the devices used, but much more important that you can comment on their effect in terms of the poem as a whole. Use a dictionary to look up any words you do not understand.

6 **Respond.** Think about why you enjoyed the poem. Was it humorous? Did it have something important to say? Was it relevant to your life? Poems mean different things to different people. Your personal response may be different from your classmates but it is just as valid.

7 **Don't worry.** Relax and enjoy as much poetry as you can. Read some for pleasure!

ISBN 9780170244213

Terminology you should be confident with ...

In Year 12 it is important to include the technical language of English in your answer. The list below is what we would expect you to know at this level.

You will notice in the left hand margin there are two circles labelled 'I know' and 'I need to check'. Read through the list and tick the box that best describes your knowledge of each literary term. Look up all the ones you don't know in the Language Lists at the end of this book.

I know	I need to check	Term
○	○	**Alliteration**
○	○	**Assonance**
○	○	**Imagery**
○	○	**Metaphor**
○	○	**Onomatopoeia**
○	○	**Personification**
○	○	**Repetition**
○	○	**Simile**

New to you may be ...

Antithesis

Placing contrasting terms or ideas close together to emphasise their difference and give the effect of balance.

For example: To err is human, to forgive, divine.
For fools rush in where angels fear to tread. (Alexander Pope)

Apostrophe

A direct address to a person or personified idea.

For example: Death, be not proud (John Donne)

Oh grave! Where is thy victory?
Oh death! Where is thy sting? (Book of Isaiah, *The Bible*)

Use of apostrophe creates the effect of a cry, an outpouring of emotion.

Caesura

A natural pause or a break in a line of poetry, usually indicated by a punctuation mark.

For example: When will the bell ring, and end this weariness?
(D.H. Lawrence, *Last Lesson of the Afternoon*)

ISBN 9780170244213

Symbolism

A word or phrase signifying a sign or mark representing something else.

For example: The dove (of peace), the cross (of Christianity)

A symbol brings a significant idea and all its connotations through use of a single word.

Oxymoron

Two words or phrases of opposite or contrasting meaning placed together for effect.

For example: Parting is such sweet sorrow.

(William Shakespeare, *Romeo and Juliet*)

This suggests that the two lovers are sad to be parting but this sadness is to be enjoyed a little as they anticipate being together again.

Enjambment

When the meaning of a line of poetry is completed on the next line.

For example: How long have they tugged the leash, and strained apart,
My pack of unruly hounds.

(D.H. Lawrence, *Last Lesson of the Afternoon*)

This technique can emphasise an idea or add to the rhythm and flow of the lines.

End-stopped line

The lines of a stanza that have a grammatical pause at the end of each line.

For example: I can haul and urge them no more.

(D.H. Lawrence, *Last Lesson of the Afternoon*)

This technique completes an idea visually and grammatically.

Sibilance

The repetition of the consonant **s** or **z** to give a hissing sound. The effect of sibilance is to slow the reader as **s** and **z** take longer to say. This, in turn, emphasises the idea and can also create an onomatopoeic effect. For example: suggesting snake-like movement and sound – '**s**lippery, **s**lithering, **s**liding **s**nake'.

ISBN 9780170244213

Rhyme

The repetition of sounds at the end of lines is **end rhyme**, while the repetition of sounds within a line is **internal rhyme**.

There are many effects that may be created through the use of rhyme. Rhyme can:

- give a musical quality to the poem
- help us to remember verses and ideas
- give us a sense of security as we know or can guess what is coming next
- shock us if we are expecting a certain rhyme and we don't get it
- make us laugh!

Rhythm

Rhythm is a natural part of our life. Our hearts beat rhythmically, our blood pulses, our lungs breathe in and out. Our seasons, months, weeks and days pass in a pattern. When we were small we liked rhythmic stories, poems, songs, rhymes.

Reading a passage aloud can help to establish its rhythm (and it may be as significant in a piece of prose as it is in a poem).

For example, in this extract from *Ulysses* by Tennyson, the long vowel sounds make the lines impossible to say quickly. The effect is one of drowsiness and lethargy:

> The long day wanes: the slow moon climbs: the deep
> Moans round with many voices ...

In contrast these lines by James Kirkup have short vowel sounds and hard consonants, to emphasise the idea of a violent storm and racing heartbeat of those experiencing it:

> Blood punches every vein,
> As lightning strips the windowpane.

The rhythm or beat of a poem is often designed to reinforce its subject matter and theme.

Extended metaphor

The comparison between two things is continued beyond the first point of comparison.

For example: How long have they tugged the leash, and strained apart,
My pack of unruly hounds! I cannot start
Them again on a quarry of knowledge they hate to hunt,

(D.H. Lawrence, *Last Lesson of the Afternoon*)

This technique extends and deepens a description.

ISBN 9780170244213

The language of poetry

To sum up, this chart draws together all of terminology you will use as you close read poetry. Use it as a reference whenever you look at an unfamiliar poem.

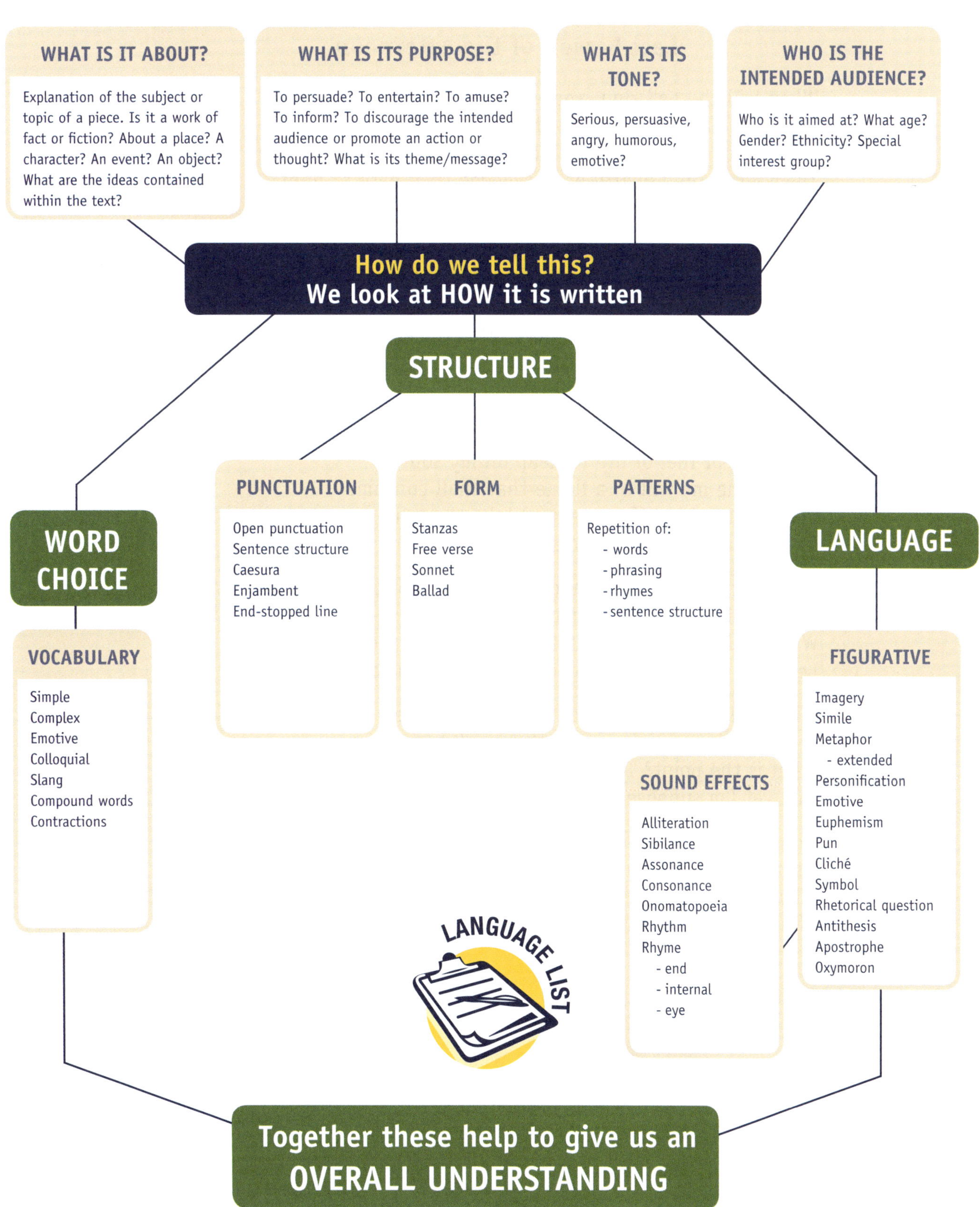

ISBN 9780170244213

Let's look at a writer's use of techniques

Some of the examples used on pages 66-68 are from this poem, *Last Lesson of the Afternoon* by D.H. Lawrence. Find them and annotate them on the page. Then look for other techniques from the chart on page 69. Note the effect of the techniques.

Last Lesson of the Afternoon

When will the bell ring, and end this weariness?
How long have they tugged the leash, and strained apart,
My pack of unruly hounds! I cannot start
Them again on a quarry of knowledge they hate to hunt,
I can haul them and urge them no more.

No longer can I endure the brunt
Of the books that lie out on the desks; a full three-score
Of several insults of blotted pages, and scrawl
Of slovenly work that they have offered me.
It is sick, and what on earth is the good of it all?
What good to them or me, I cannot see!

So, shall I take
My last dear fuel of life to heap on my soul
And kindle my will to a flame that shall consume
Their dross of indifference; and take the toll
Of their insults in punishment? – I will not! –

I will not waste my soul and my strength for this.
What do I care for all that they do amiss!
What is the point of this teaching of mine, and of this
Learning of theirs? It all goes down the same abyss.

What does it matter to me, if they can write
A description of a dog, or if they can't?
What is the point? To us both, it is all my aunt!
And yet I'm supposed to care, with all my might.

I do not, and will not; they won't and they don't; and that's all!
I shall keep my strength for myself; they can keep theirs as well.
Why should we beat our heads against the wall
Of each other? I shall sit and wait for the bell.

D.H. Lawrence

See how the poet's techniques work together to create an effective description of a significant moment in his life. Lawrence did not teach for long!

ISBN 9780170244213

Annotating a poem

A useful way of trying to understand and appreciate a poem is to place a copy of it in the middle of a sheet of paper and annotate your ideas around it.

1 Read the poem aloud if possible, or alternatively listen to someone else read it.
2 Read the poem to yourself several more times as you get confident with its vocabulary, rhythm and flow.
3 Using a quality dictionary, look up the meaning of any words you are unsure of. Annotate these definitions. A dictionary often gives several meanings for a word so you need to pick the meaning that fits the poem.

Look for:

4 the subject
5 the poet's attitude towards the subject, often revealed as 'tone'
6 the theme.

Then look for:

7 images, created by use of figures of speech perhaps
8 effective words (diction, vocabulary)
9 patterns like sentence structure, verses, rhyme.

Then ask yourself:

10 what do I think about the poem and its ideas?

An aside on ... what will you be asked about?

At this level you will be asked to close read an unseen poem. Poetry offers examiners a concise text, while a poem's form lends itself to being an excellent model of language, vocabulary choice and imagery. Although there are features common to all texts, it is likely that any analysis you do on poetry in particular will ask questions similar to this one ...

1 Analyse how the writer uses particular techniques to develop the idea that ...

Techniques might include simile, metaphor, onomatopoeia etc.

Support your answer with specific details from the text, and explain how these details work to develop ideas.

In your answer you should:

- identify and give examples of techniques and explain their effects
- show understanding of the ideas the writer is communicating
- show understanding of the writer's overall purpose.

ISBN 9780170244213

Let's look at a poem together

Here is a well-known New Zealand poem, *Farmhand*, by James K. Baxter. It has been annotated for you.

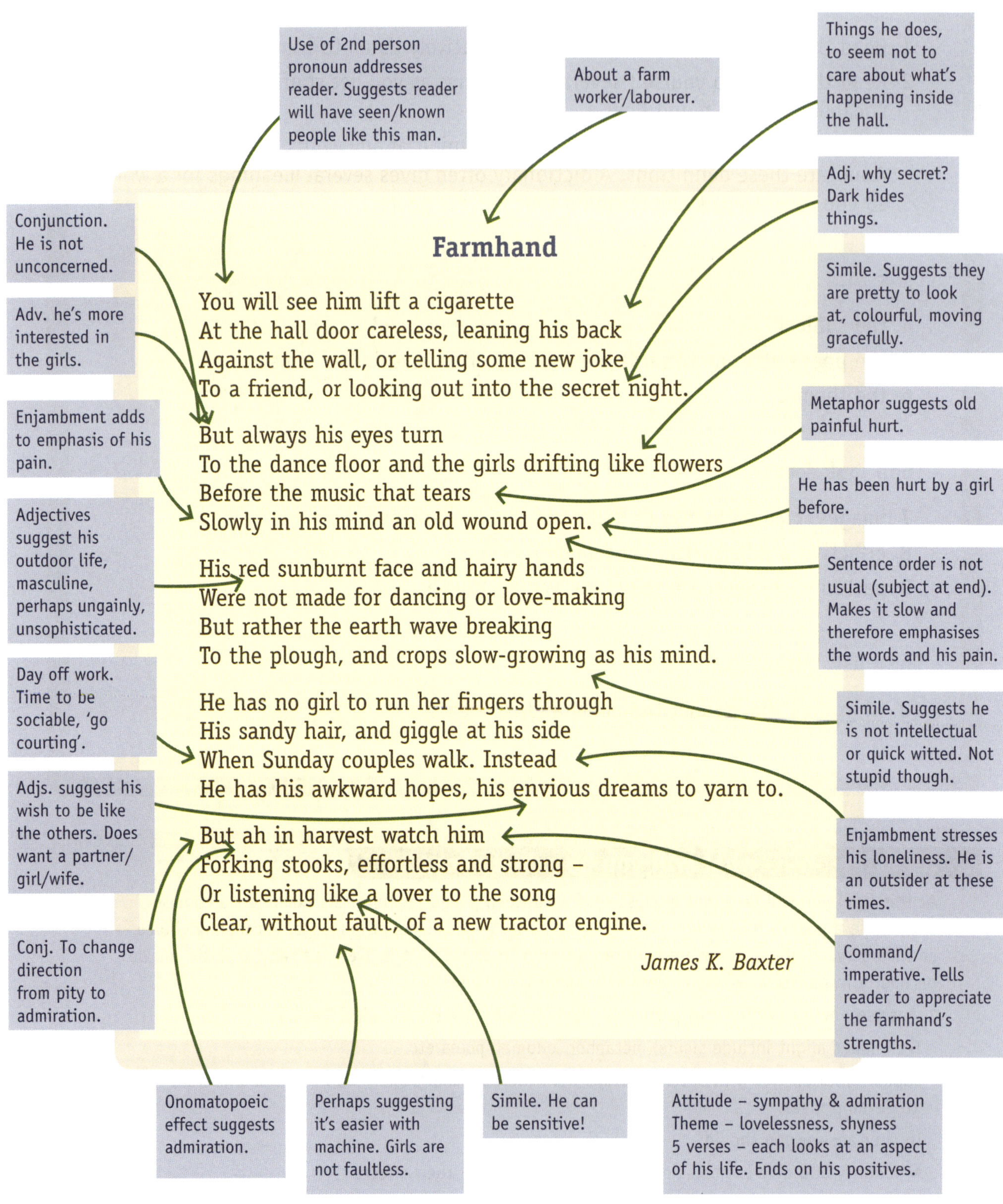

Farmhand

You will see him lift a cigarette
At the hall door careless, leaning his back
Against the wall, or telling some new joke
To a friend, or looking out into the secret night.

But always his eyes turn
To the dance floor and the girls drifting like flowers
Before the music that tears
Slowly in his mind an old wound open.

His red sunburnt face and hairy hands
Were not made for dancing or love-making
But rather the earth wave breaking
To the plough, and crops slow-growing as his mind.

He has no girl to run her fingers through
His sandy hair, and giggle at his side
When Sunday couples walk. Instead
He has his awkward hopes, his envious dreams to yarn to.

But ah in harvest watch him
Forking stooks, effortless and strong –
Or listening like a lover to the song
Clear, without fault, of a new tractor engine.

James K. Baxter

ISBN 9780170244213

Now you will be able to write an appreciation of this poem, explaining the things we have noticed. A space has been left for you to try this. The headings will help you to structure your appreciation of the poem. Remember the poem is a whole creation so everything will link to the meaning, and always use references to and quotations from the poem to support your ideas.

1 The subject of the poem is ______

2 The poet has chosen some effective ______

3 The poet is suggesting that the farmhand ______

4 I like/dislike this poem because ______

Poetry close reading practice

A variety of poetic text and accompanying questions are provided in this section to help you practise your close reading questions.

Text 1

Read the following poem. Annotate important features (see pages 65-71).

Use a dictionary to look up the following words:

- stampeding
- wielded
- scaled
- brunt

Wind

This house has been far out at sea all night,
The woods crashing through darkness, the booming hills,
Winds stampeding the fields under the window
Floundering black astride and blinding wet

Till day rose; then under an orange sky
The hills had new places, and wind wielded
Blade-light, luminous and emerald,
Flexing like the lens of a mad eye.

At noon I scaled along the house-side as far as
The coal-house door. Once I looked up –
Through the brunt wind that dented the balls of my eyes
The tent of the hills drummed and strained its guyrope,

The fields quivering, the skyline a grimace,
At any second to bang and vanish with a flap:
The wind flung a magpie away and a black-
Back gull bent like an iron bar slowly. The house

Rang like some fine green goblet in the note
That any second would shatter it. Now deep
In chairs, in front of the great fire, we grip
Our hearts and cannot entertain book, thought,

Or each other. We watch the fire blazing,
And feel the roots of the house move, but sit on,
Seeing the window tremble to come in,
Hearing the stones cry out under the horizons.

Ted Hughes

ISBN 9780170244213

Answer the following questions in as much detail as possible:

1 What is the subject of this poem?

2 The opening line uses a figure of speech. What is it and why has the poet chosen it?

3 Explain the difference in focus between verses 1 and 2. How are the two verses linked?

4 In verse 3 comment on the use of the words 'scaled' and 'dented'.

5 Comment on the rhythm of lines 15 and 16.

6 How does the poet reveal the feelings of the people in the final two verses?

7 Explain what you think the theme of this poem is. Use at least **two** references to poetic technique in your answer.

ISBN 9780170244213

Text 2

Read the following poem. Annotate important features (see pages 65-71).

Use a dictionary to look up the following words:

- wrenched
- succumbs
- pursed
- drear

Friend

Do you remember
that wild stretch of land
with the lone tree guarding the point
from the sharp-tongued sea?

The fort we built out of branches
wrenched from the tree is dead wood now.
The air that was thick with the whirr of
toetoe spear succumbs at last to the grey gull's wheel.

Oyster-studded roots
of the mangrove yield no finer feast
of silver-bellied eels, and sea-snails
cooked in a rusty can.

Allow me to mend the broken ends
of shared days:
but I wanted to say
that the tree we climbed
that gave food and drink
to youthful dreams, is no more.
Pursed to the lips her fine-edged
leaves made whistle - now stamp
no silken tracery on the cracked
clay floor.

Friend,
in this drear
dreamless time I clasp
your hand if only to reassure
that all our jewelled fantasies were
real and wore splendid rags.

Perhaps the tree
will strike fresh roots again:
give soothing shade to a hurt and
troubled world.

Hone Tuwhare

ISBN 9780170244213

Answer the following questions in as much detail as possible:

1 To whom is the poem addressed? How can you tell?

2 Choose an example of the following techniques and explain the effect created by each one.

i Personification

ii Alliteration

iii Effective verb

iv Emotive adjective

3 What does the poet remember about their shared past? Comment on the poet's references to dreams.

4 What does the final verse suggest to you?

Text 3

Read the following poem. Annotate important features (see pages 65-71).

Use a dictionary to look up the following words:

- Suspension
- plunge
- braced
- rivets

The Diver

The bridge like a Roman fort
held the river and the beach
held our vision steady through waving heat
held us all while the solitary figure
struggled up the arch
his knees braced against the rivets
Below someone shook out his towel
while others bet upon his chance
At the summit of the span he rose
his arms outstretched
flung a cross against the sun
and the whole world hung beneath him
our eyes nailing him to the sky
Suspension for an instant and forever
A slow plunge toward the water
and he came down from above
dropping beneath the surface like a stone
The river circling away
grew silent as held breath
  still as death
Then from unknown depths
his head broke the water
shook out a crown of sunlit spray
brought release   new life
thrilling our chest.

Robert Currie

ISBN 9780170244213

Answer the following questions in as much detail as possible:

1 In about 20 words describe the literal chain of events in this poem.

____

____

____

2 The poem draws an analogy with another significant, well-known event. Explain the analogy and choose **three** images that reveal the analogy.

____

____

____

____

3 Examine the impact of the use of repetition in lines 2, 3, and 4.

____

____

4 The poet uses no punctuation. How does he shape his poem?

____

____

____

5 Parts of speech: Choose one effective verb and one effective adjective in the poem. Explain why each one is effective.

Verb ______________ Effect ______________________

____

Adjective ______________ Effect ______________________

____

6 Figures of speech: Identify an example of use of alliteration, metaphor and simile from the poem. Choose **one** and explain why the poet chose to use it.

Alliteration ______________________________________

Metaphor ____

Simile ____

Explanation ______________________________________

____

____

____

ISBN 9780170244213

Text 4

Read the following poem. Annotate important features (see pages 65-71).

Use a dictionary to look up the following words:

- *stealth*
- *coy*
- *haberdashery*
- *bloodhound*
- *frail*

Hat

Dad wouldn't be seen dead
without a hat.
Farm hat, summer hat, town hat
even when he had hair.

Hat on an angle, hat on horse,
hat in the truck with dogs.

We fished by stealth
stalked trout
with a spear and a light.
He wore his hat in the dark.

A mile apart by metal road
my grandmother lived
on her half of the farm.
No chance meetings, not even
a skyline sighting.

She lay in wait in town
watched
from the haberdashery
as he walked up the street.
She came out as if by accident.
Hand frail, and clasping
the front of her coat,
she gave a coy look
from the bags of her bloodhound eyes—
the whole air stopped

he raised his hat, went past.

Marty Smith

ISBN 9780170244213

Answer the following questions in as much detail as possible:

1 Identify the language feature in the opening two lines and explain its meaning.

2 What is suggested by line 4?

3 Why does the narrator mention hats so many times in the first three verses?

4 What is suggested about the family circumstances in the fourth verse?

5 Who is 'She' in verse 5? What is she doing?

6 What is the narrator's attitude towards her? How can you tell?

7 Why is there a space between the end of verse 5 and the final line of the poem?

8 What is the significance of the man's actions in the final line?

ISBN 9780170244213

Text 5

Read the following poem. Annotate important features (see pages 65-71).

If you like, you can look up Colin McCahon's poster on the Internet.

Use a dictionary to look up the following words:

- *phlegmatic*
- *stutter*
- *memoirs*
- *pneumatic*

A Winter Christmas

Our flat's attacked by tinsel. It steals
Across the walls, clinging
by tiny pads of blue-tac. A silver
caterpillar eyes the African violet
while its phlegmatic cousin creeps above
the McCahon* poster we've carried all the way
from home. *Tomorrow will be the same*
but not as this is. Out on Gray's Inn Road**
they're digging up the road. Pneumatic drills
stutter below our vase of winter daffodils,
snow falls but apparently won't settle.
All day pigeons fly in and out
of the upper windows of the Royal Free Hospital,**
and late at night you sense a hint of wind,
probably some stars. The various sounds
of ambulance and fire drift up ...
A voice or two, one calling *police*
or *please*, then footsteps vanishing.
Dark night, dark traffic, probably some stars.
England alone with her memoirs,
reading the children off to sleep.

Bill Manhire

*Colin McCahon, NZ painter
**places in central London

ISBN 9780170244213

Answer the following questions in as much detail as possible:

1 Where and when is the poem set? Refer to the text to support your response.

2 Is this the poet's usual residence? How does he suggest this place is different from his home?

3 What does the poem suggest to you about how the poet is feeling?

4 Explain the final two lines of the poem.

Text 6

Read the following poem. Annotate important features (see pages 65-71).

You can find the famous photograph Bruce Dawe talks about on the Internet. Use clues from the poem to help you.

Use a dictionary to look up the following words:

- madonnas
- lustrous
- aesthetic balance
- wasted
- harmony
- coalesce
- imponderable
- litany

The Sadness of Madonnas

On the famous news-photo of an Ethiopian mother and child

The sadness of madonnas is that they
at times too easily satisfy
our hunger for aesthetic balance, our deep craving
for harmony in hell — the eyes look sideways down,
pondering imponderable mysteries, such as where
the next meal's coming from, the robe
frayed at the edges frames the high-cheekboned face;
her grave full lips, if they could speak,
would utter (so we think) such other-worldly wisdom
as we're familiar with (suffering ennobles; this present
vale of tears is, after all, not *all;* He will not ask us
to bear above what we are able ...)
Admittedly, the arms are far too thin
for comfort, bony fingers
framing the child's large skull
suggest the truth which plainly speaks
in the lustrous eyes, the xylophone
rib-cage and the wasted
music of leg-bones — such images
separate, and blur, and coalesce
in the terrible litany of particulars:
the thousands lying silent in the dirt,
the dehydrated children's skin as tough as leather,
the little fingers creeping out for comfort,
the grieving hearts that hold them ...

Bruce Dawe

ISBN 9780170244213

Answer the following questions in as much detail as possible:

1 The first 11 lines of the poem speak mostly of the religious Madonna figure and her role in our world. Explain that role and say why this woman is called a madonna.

2 Which words tell you that this woman has a different focus from the Madonna figure that the poet compares her with?

3 Which word divides the poem into its second part? What is the poet's focus here?

4 How can you tell the child is starving?

5 How does the poet reveal the difference between the religious Madonna figure and this woman?

ISBN 9780170244213

Something a little different - SONNETS

Many of you will have read some of Shakespeare's plays in your English class but did you know that he was also a poet? Shakespeare wrote 154 poems in sonnet form, dealing with themes such as the passage of time, love, beauty and mortality.

Here are some very important facts about the careful STRUCTURE of a Shakespearian sonnet:

- They are almost all constructed from three four-line stanzas (called quatrains) and a final rhyming couplet.
- Each quatrain develops a specific idea, but one closely related to the ideas in the other quatrains.
- They are composed in iambic pentameter (a meter used extensively in Shakespeare's plays).
- They follow the same rhyme scheme - abab cdcd efef gg.
- There is a turn between the third quatrain and the concluding couplet.
- The concluding rhyming couplet acts as a conclusion and often gives the meaning or purpose of the sonnet.

If you have studied **Romeo and Juliet** you will know that both the Prologue and the Epilogue are sonnets.

Here, more than anything we want you to understand that Shakespeare's language is English, and you **can** understand what he is saying.

Take a look at one of his sonnets. Read it aloud several times.

SONNET 55

Not marble, nor the gilded monuments
Of princes, shall outlive this powerful rhyme;
But you shall shine more bright in these contents
Than unswept stone besmear'd with sluttish time.
When wasteful war shall statues overturn,
And broils root out the work of masonry,
Nor Mars his sword nor war's quick fire shall burn
The living record of your memory.
'Gainst death and all-oblivious enmity
Shall you pace forth; your praise shall still find room
Even in the eyes of all posterity
That wear this world out to the ending doom.
So, till the judgment that yourself arise,
You live in this, and dwell in lovers' eyes.

Much has been written about Shakespeare and his poetry. If you are interested you could find out about his reasons for writing his sonnets.

Having a hard time understanding this? Let's see if we can help you out ...

ISBN 9780170244213

SONNET 55	PARAPHRASE
Not marble, nor the gilded monuments	Not marble, nor the gold-plated shrines
Of princes, shall outlive this powerful rhyme;	Of princes shall outlive the power of poetry;
But you shall shine more bright in these contents	You shall shine brightly in these verses
Than unswept stone besmear'd with sluttish time.	Than on dust-covered gravestones, ravaged by filthy time.
When wasteful war shall statues overturn,	When devastating war overturns statues,
And broils root out the work of masonry,	And conflicts destroy the mason's handiwork,
Nor Mars his sword nor war's quick fire shall burn	the cause of war (Mars) nor the effects of war (fire) shall destroy
The living record of your memory.	The living record of your memory (this poem).
'Gainst death and all-oblivious enmity	Against death & destruction, which means people get forgotten
Shall you pace forth; your praise shall still find room	You will push onward; praise of you will always find a place,
Even in the eyes of all posterity	Even in the eyes of future generations
That wear this world out to the ending doom.	That survive until the end of humanity.
So, till the judgement that yourself arise,	So, until you arise on Judgement Day,
You live in this, and dwell in lovers' eyes.	You are immortalised in this poetry, and continue to live in lovers' eyes.

1 On either version of the sonnet annotate the following features:
- Each four-line stanza (quatrain)
- The final couplet
- The rhyme scheme - abab cdcd efef gg.

2 As explained earlier each stanza/quatrain develops a specific idea. In your own words explain the idea developed in each.

Stanza/quatrain 1 ______________________________

____

Stanza/quatrain 2 ______________________________

____

Stanza/quatrain 3 ______________________________

____

Stanza/quatrain 4 ______________________________

____

3 The concluding rhyming couplet acts as a conclusion and often gives the meaning or purpose of the sonnet. What is the key idea of *Sonnet 55*?

____

____

ISBN 9780170244213

Let's see what you can do on your own

Now you have seen one of Shakespeare's sonnets paraphrased we'd like you to try to paraphrase a very famous one yourself. We have given you a detailed set of footnotes to make this easier for you. Using a thesaurus can help too.

SONNET 18	PARAPHRASE
Shall I compare thee to a summer's day?	
Thou art more lovely and more temperate.	
Rough winds do shake the darling buds of May,	
And summer's lease hath all too short a date:	
Sometime too hot the eye of heaven shines,	
And often is his gold complexion dimmed,	
And every fair from fair sometime declines,	
By chance, or nature's changing course untrimmed:	
But thy eternal summer shall not fade,	
Nor lose possession of that fair thou ow'st,	
Nor shall death brag thou wander'st in his shade,	
When in eternal lines to time thou grow'st,	
So long as men can breathe, or eyes can see,	
So long lives this, and this gives life to thee.	

FOOTNOTES

2: temperate = mild, gentle, restrained, evenly-tempered; not overcome by passion.
3: darling buds = most loved, beautiful, favourite.
4: summer's = youth's, summer season.
4: lease = allowance, in the sense of the time allowed for something; allotted time.
4: too short = too soon.
4: date = date of expiration, duration.
5: sometime = on occasion, sometimes.
5: eye of heaven = the Sun.
6: gold = refers to both the classic colour of the Sun, and also implies 'value.'
6: complexion = mood, face.
7: every fair = all beautiful things.
7: from fair = from everything beautiful.
7: declines = falls, declines.
8: changing = change-causing.
8: untrimm'd = unslowed; nautical metaphor, from the practice of trimming sail to slow a ship; or stripped of ornament and decoration.
9: fade = darken; so as to be lost from sight.
10: fair = beauty.
10: ow'st = ownest, possess.
11: shade = darkness.
12: lines = lines of this poem.
12: to time = into the future.
12: grow'st = flourish.
13: breathe = to be able to speak.
14: this = that.

ISBN 9780170244213

Now that you have worked out what the sonnet says, let's check you understand it ...

1 On either version of the sonnet annotate the following features:

- Each four-line stanza (quatrain)
- The final couplet
- The rhyme scheme - abab cdcd efef gg.

2 As explained earlier each stanza/quatrain develops a specific idea. In your own words explain the idea developed in each.

Stanza/quatrain 1 ______________________________

____

____

Stanza/quatrain 2 ______________________________

____

____

Stanza/quatrain 3 ______________________________

____

____

Stanza/quatrain 4 ______________________________

____

____

3 If you were the person to whom the poem is addressed would you agree with its sentiments?

____

____

____

____

____

____

____

ISBN 9780170244213

7 Text type 3: Visual

Visual text is a prominent means of communication in today's world. Every day you see pictures that are trying to communicate with you:

- billboards on the street
- pictures in newspapers and magazines
- CD and DVD covers
- advertising in stores, on the Internet, even on buses
- T-shirts and banners towed by aircraft.

An aside on ... why we are getting you to look at visual text

Although you may not directly be assessed on visual texts in your external examinations it is still a valuable skill to learn. We know that many students enjoy this sort of analysis because they see these images around them all the time in their everyday life. Many of the techniques used in the creation of visual images are the same or similar to those used in written text – often because the visual incorporates words as well as pictures.

That is worth repeating: most of these 'pictures' are in fact a mixture of words and images and we refer to the techniques you will use to analyse as visual language.

For many of you, your knowledge of visual communication will have come from designing and producing a visual piece for assessment. In the close reading of visual text the focus changes slightly. While you are still expected to be aware of the techniques used to create the image, it is more likely the questions will focus on the language content or ideas within the image.

At this more senior level, the most distinctive change will be the increasing sophistication of the images you are required to respond to.

This is a section examining your ability to read, understand and appreciate rather than to create.

ISBN 9780170244213

Terminology you should be confident with...

In Year 12 it is important to include the technical language of English in your answer. The list below is what we would expect you to know at this level.

You will notice in the left hand margin there are two circles labelled 'I know' and 'I need to check'. Read through the list and tick the box that best describes your knowledge of each literary term. Look up all the ones you don't know in the Language Lists at the end of this book.

Verbal techniques

I know	I need to check	
○	○	Alliteration
○	○	Cliché
○	○	Emotive language
○	○	Hyperbole
○	○	Imperative
○	○	Personal pronoun
○	○	Pun
○	○	Repetition
○	○	Rhetorical question
○	○	Slogan
○	○	Tone
○	○	Use of adjectives

Visual techniques

I know	I need to check	
○	○	Graphic/Illustration
○	○	Bold lines
○	○	Colour
○	○	Contrast
○	○	Font (style and size)
○	○	Logos
○	○	Reverse print
○	○	Symbols
○	○	Unusual images
○	○	Well-known people

Layout

I know	I need to check	
○	○	Balance
○	○	Borders
○	○	DVF
○	○	Empty space
○	○	Hierarchy
○	○	Perspective
○	○	Proportion
○	○	Rule of thirds

New to you may be ...

Acronym

A pronounceable word created by taking the initial letters of a series of words.
For example: SADD = Students Against Drunk Driving
ANZAC = Australia New Zealand Army Corps

Caricature

Characterisation that exaggerates certain features for comic effect.

ISBN 9780170244213

An aside on ... eye movement

Not surprisingly, advertising agencies are interested in how their work is viewed/read by the public and have carried out market research themselves to discover how the average reader behaves. One method is described below.

A reader starts first with the illustration.

After the picture the reader's eye goes to the headline. It is from here that the advertiser will need to work to hold the attention.

The reader's eye then moves to the bottom, usually the right-hand corner, and this is commonly where the company brand name is positioned. It does not have to be big but it is important to leave it uncluttered, so other important details (contact details, etc) are more likely to be found at the end of the body copy.

It is likely that any small type around or under the picture will then be read, or any smaller illustrations are looked at more closely.

The reader will then 'flirt' with the body copy by reading the first sentence/line. The key is to hook the reader into the rest of the paragraph by writing in an interesting manner. That way, readers will follow the argument to the last full stop.

Look at this advertisement. How did you 'read' it?

ISBN 9780170244213

The language of visuals

To sum up, this chart draws together all of terminology you will use as you close read visual text. Use it as a reference whenever you look at a piece of unfamiliar visual text.

ELEMENTS OF A VISUAL TEXT

AUDIENCE

Who is the image aimed at? What age group? Gender? Ethnicity or consumer group?

PURPOSE

Does it grab attention? Does it try to influence us to act a certain way or make a particular decision?

MESSAGE

What is it saying? What are the ideas contained within the image?

Features of Design (Visual and verbal)

COLOUR

Does it create:
- contrast?
- impact?
- mood?

Is the colour representative?

Red	White	Black
danger	purity	death
love	clean	elegance
blood	fresh	sophistication

Blue	Yellow	Green
water	spring	envy
tranquillity	youth	new life
		nature

Warm colours move forward visually.
Cold colours move back visually.

TEXTURE

Does it:
- Give variety to the design?
- Add depth?
- Represent mood?
- Make you 'feel' something?

LAYOUT

Is it effective?
Has the designer thought about:
- a focal point
- border
- balance
- empty space
- contrast
- hierarchy
- perspective
- proportion
- rule of thirds

How have the verbal and visual elements been put together?

LETTERING

One word?
Catch phrase?
Body copy?
A combination?

Is the font appropriate to the subject? Mood?

Are the letters clear?
Bold? Italicised?
Superimposed?

ILLUSTRATION/GRAPHIC

How does it make you feel?
Does it give us a message?
Carries some information?

Is it provoking? Funny?
Unusual? Dramatic? Shocking?
Controversial?

LANGUAGE TECHNIQUES

What language techniques has the designer used to help get the message across or reach the desired audience?

Grammar
statements
contractions
sentence structure

Vocabulary
repetition
new words (neologisms)
slang
jargon
personal pronouns

Tone
formal/colloquial/authoritative/threatening/romantic

Clever use of words
clichés/puns/hyperbole/alliteration/neologisms/rhyme/onomatopoeia/emotive language/rhetorical question/commands (imperative)

LANGUAGE LIST

Together these give us OVERALL IMPACT

Making it stand out in a crowd.
Does it catch your eye?
Do you want to buy the product?

Making it noticeable, and therefore memorable.
Do you do a doubletake?
Does it prompt action? Does it make you think?

ISBN 9780170244213

Test your knowledge

Look carefully at this visual text and complete the chart on the opposite page.

Do you want to work in a place where people know how to have fun? Are you looking for your first job, a career in hospitality and some extra cash? Swing by your nearest Burger King restaurant and check out the fired up career opportunities or you can e-mail jobs@bknz.co.nz From here the only way is up!

Pride ! Passion ! Performance !

ISBN 9780170244213

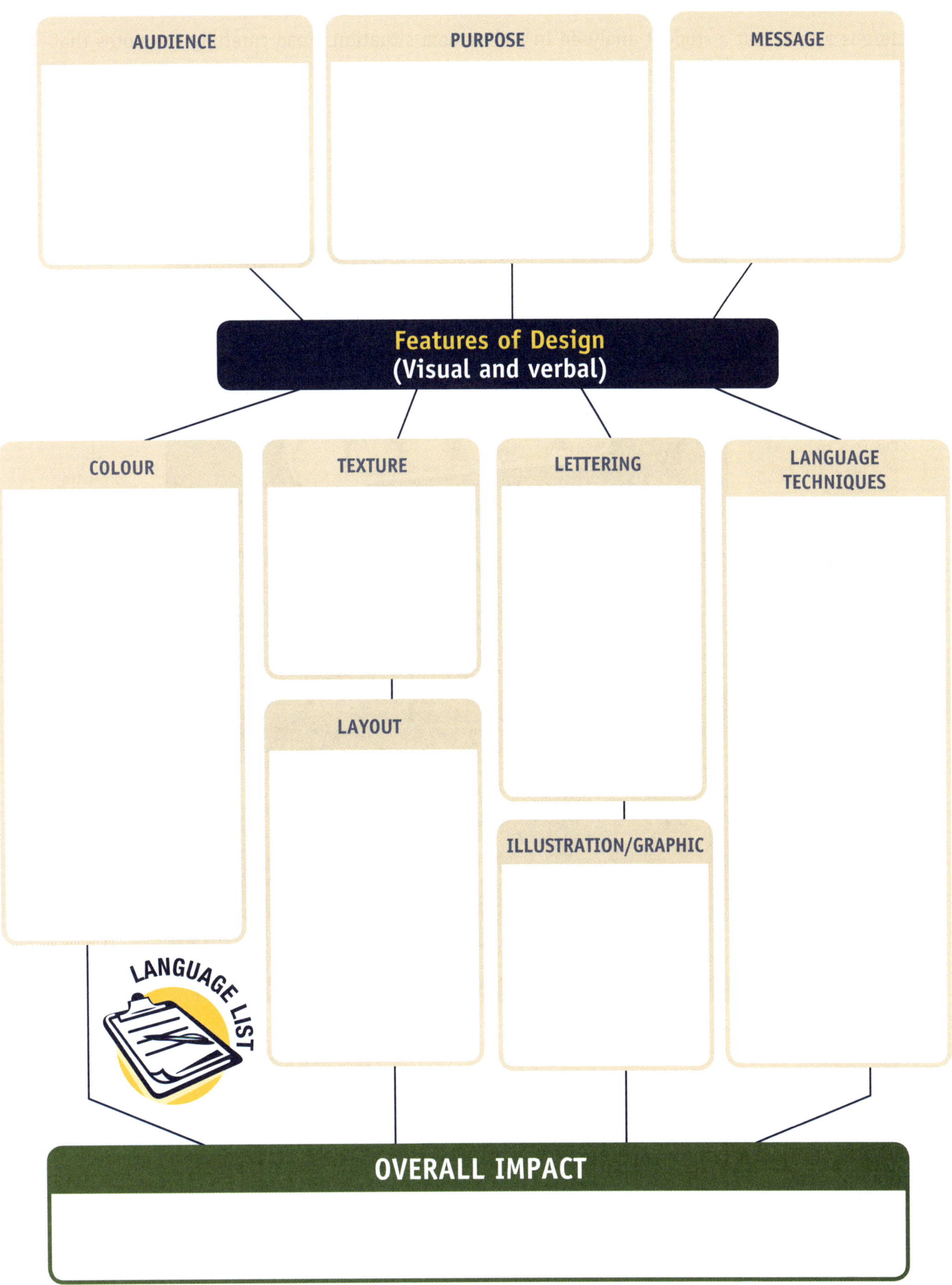

ISBN 9780170244213

Let's look at a student's first thoughts on a visual text

Here is a text that a student analysed in a classroom situation. Read carefully the notes that surround the advertisement.

Font:
- easy/simple to read
- formal ... suits topic
- change of size = importance
- 1½ space of smaller writing makes it easy to read

A – eggs ... black
I – headline
D – desire to help
A – pledge/website

Illustration:
soft, comforting, supportive package.
Eggs are treated carefully but not the hens.

Headline:
Makes you think.
Makes you read on.
Connects to picture of eggs at top and hens below.

Emotive language:
- crammed
- tiny
- painful
- suffers
- pecked
- frustrated
- mutilated
- hell
- denied
- madness

Personal pronouns 'She' and 'Her' make the hen appear 'human'/'real'.

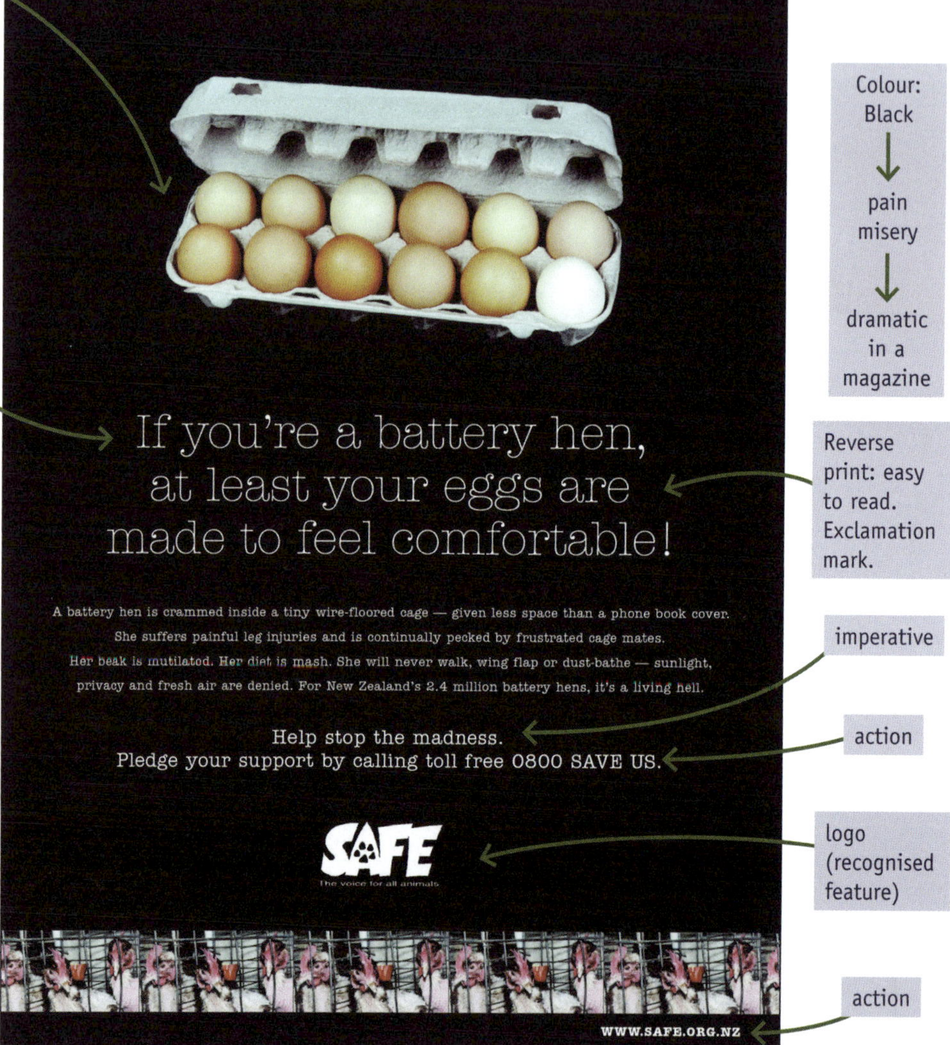

Colour:
Black
↓
pain
misery
↓
dramatic in a magazine

Reverse print: easy to read.
Exclamation mark.

imperative

action

logo (recognised feature)

action

Strip pictures:
Shows conditions that they live in.
Same repeated picture highlights how many (2.2 million hens).
Gives an 'edge' to poster.
Balances top illustration.
Makes us look closely.

Language:
Compound word – wire-floor
Personal pronoun – you're/your, she/her
Statistics – 2.2 million
Alliteration – ... will never walk, wing flap ...
Cliché – living hell

ISBN 9780170244213

Use the annotation supplied to answer the following questions on the image. The notes surrounding the advertisement will help you to give detailed responses.

1 Comment on the type of language the advertiser has chosen to use in order to get their message across.

2 What is the connection between the images and the lead sentence, 'If you're a battery hen, at least your eggs are made to feel comfortable!'?

3 Comment on the reasons behind the use of colour in this advertisement.

ISBN 9780170244213

Visual close reading practice

A variety of visual text and accompanying questions are provided in this section to help you practise your close reading.

Text 1

Read the following advertisement. Annotate important features (see page 93).

ISBN 9780170244213

Before you go further ...

Complete the following chart.

What is it **about**?	What is the **purpose**?	What is the **message**?	Who is the **audience**?

Answer the following questions in as much detail as possible:

1 The writer has played on the idea of the water being both New Zealand in origin and natural. Write down the words/phrases that relate to:

a New Zealand ______________________________

____

____

b nature ______________________________

____

____

2 The writer has also alluded to the quality of the product. Which words/phrases are used to suggest Kiwi Blue is a superior product to others on the market?

____

____

____

____

____

____

____

____

An aside on ... laughter

Some advertisements are just plain clever. They can make you laugh and often they have only two or three words on them. You probably won't find many of this sort of advertisement in a textbook or as a text in an English examination because in the end there is little to analyse, but a chapter on advertising would not be complete without acknowledging the cleverness of some of the people working in this field. Why don't you try and find a funny or witty advertisement!

ISBN 9780170244213

Text 2

Read the following advertisement. Annotate important features (see page 93).

OPEN A BOTTLE OF CODORNÍU AND IT'S HISTORY.

A family history that dates back to the early sixteenth century. In 1551 Jaime Codorniu left a will and testament bequeathing wine cellars, presses, barrels and vats to his heirs. And so began a great wine-making dynasty.

Codorniu produced their first bottle of sparkling wine in the early 1870s, using methods and techniques discovered in France. This new "methode champenoise", known in Spain as "Cava" received wide acclaim, and in the years to come would win several gold medals at the world's finest wine festivals.

Four centuries later, there are now some 100 million bottles of Codorniu Cava housed beneath the estate in the sixteen miles of cellars.

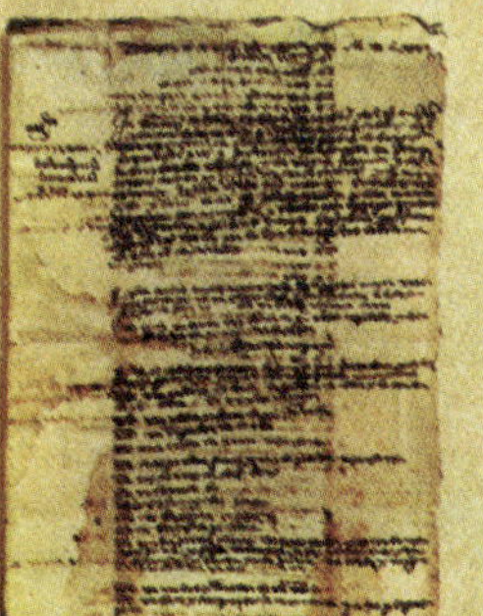

It's here that the wine undergoes the crucial stage of bottle fermentation. Languishing for up to five years in the controlled temperatures, the cool slow fermentation produces a fine delicate sparkle and a characteristic taste.

It's a taste that can be enjoyed anytime, day or night. Relax with friends over a well-chilled bottle one sunny afternoon. Or add a touch of romance to your next dinner party.

And for a special treat simply add one or two fresh strawberries to a tall champagne flute of Codorniu - it's a taste even Jaime Codorniu himself would approve of.

Since the early sixteenth century, Codorniu has been raised in toast by kings and queens, presidents and personalities the world over - King Juan Carlos of Spain, Queen Margareth of Denmark and King Karl-Gustav of Sweden to name just a few.

And from around $12.95 a bottle, you won't need a King's ransom to try it.

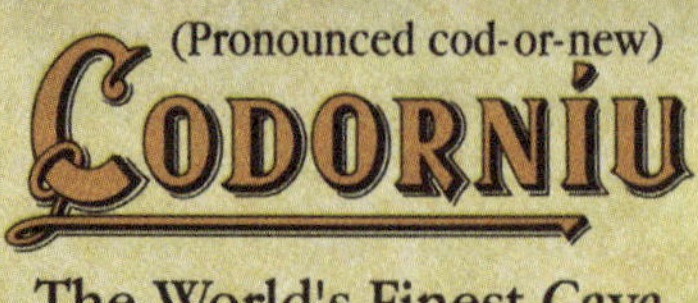

ISBN 9780170244213

Before you go further ...

Complete the following chart.

What is it **about**?	What is the **purpose**?	What is the **message**?	Who is the **audience**?

Answer the following questions in as much detail as possible:

1 Explain the relevance of the apostrophe used in the headline.

2 Find two examples of the use of imperatives. Explain why they are used.

i

ii

3 List words/phrases from the body copy that build up the concept of 'dynasty'.

4 Emotive language is used to make the product sound like it is the best quality. Give five examples of emotive language and explain how each one helps build up this impression of quality.

i

ii

ISBN 9780170244213

iii

iv

v

5 Explain how the use of colour and illustrations relate to the text.

ISBN 9780170244213

Text 3

Read the following advertisement. Annotate important features (see page 93).

To bring you the plumpest, juiciest grapes in the world, we nourish them, nurture them, pamper them and when no-one's looking we even talk to them.

Then we squash em.

It seems a shame doesn't it. To put all that effort into raising the most succulent grapes known to mankind, just to squish them when they reach the peak of perfection. Still, what's a little squeeze between friends, especially when the end product is possibly the most luscious dark grape juice your taste buds will ever experience. What they won't experience is sugar or preservatives because the only thing that goes into our dark grape juice is dark grape juice.

ISBN 9780170244213

Before you go further ...

Complete the following chart.

What is it **about**?	What is the **purpose**?	What is the **message**?	Who is the **audience**?

Answer the following questions in as much detail as possible:

1 Comment on the main illustration and how it relates to the text of the advertisement.

2 Identify the language techniques in 'squash em' and 'squish them' and comment on why they are effective.

3 Comment on the use of the small illustration of a juice carton, glass of juice and grapes at the bottom left-hand corner of the advertisement and why this type of illustration is commonly used in advertising.

ISBN 9780170244213

4 Identify two other language techniques that appear in the advertisement and comment on their effects.

i

ii

5 In your opinion is this advertisement successful? Refer to both verbal and visual features in your answer.

Something a little different - HOW A STUDENT USED WHAT THEY HAD LEARNT

Let's have a look at how a Year 12 student used the same language techniques we have discussed in this section to create their own product blurb. The task was to create a suitable and consistent tone through language choice. Highlight and annotate as many techniques as you can find.

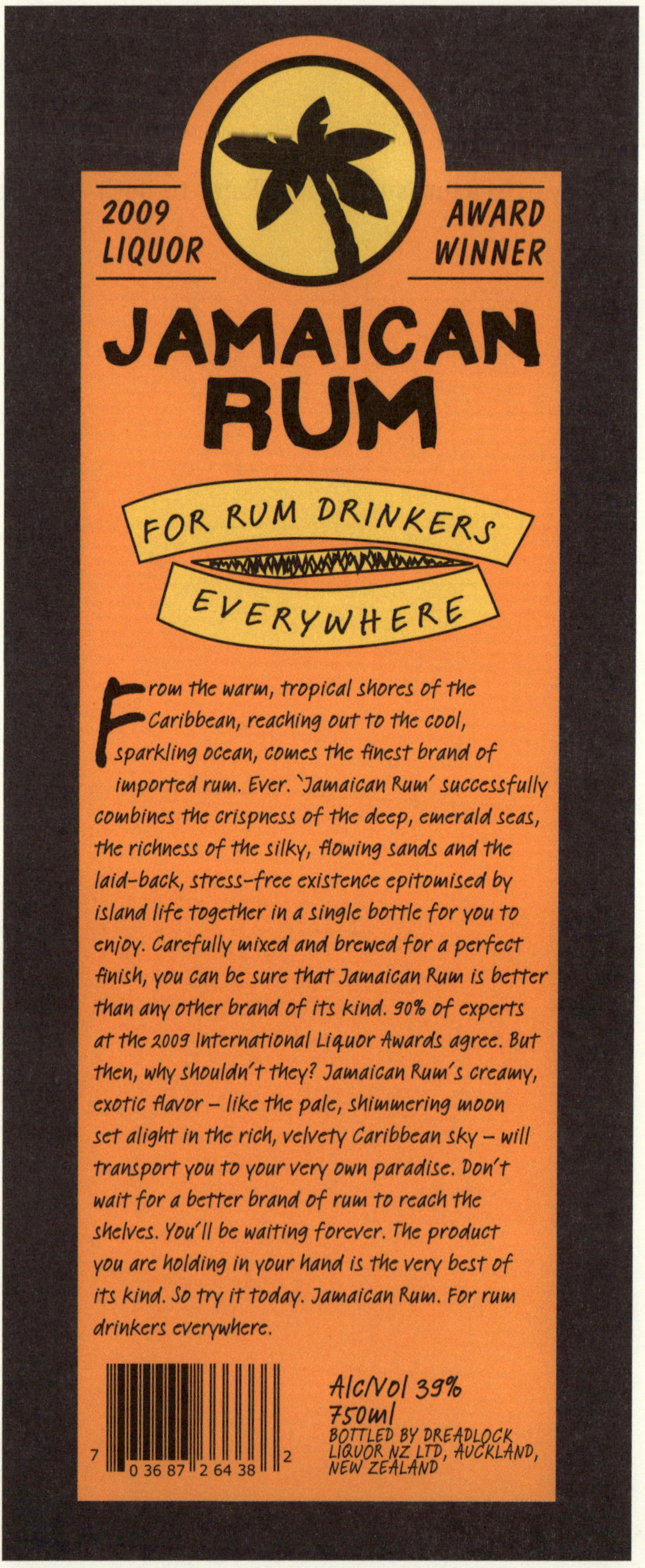

ISBN 9780170244213

D.I.Y.

Using language techniques yourself to create a consistent tone to advertise a product or service can help you identify and appreciate language techniques in other texts.

So let's see what you can do.

Select a product or service and produce an appropriate blurb. Draft the text and then put the final version on this page. Annotate it, showing where your techniques have been used. Or swap with your neighbour and annotate each other's.

ISBN 9780170244213

8 Text type 4: Oral

An oral text is one that is meant to be spoken. It may be an extract from a play for stage, screen or radio. It may be the transcript of a conversation, a speech or a debate. It may be the words of an advertisement, a sermon or a song.

The delivery of an oral text is very important and hearing the way the words are spoken helps us to fully understand and appreciate their meaning. In some situations, seeing the delivery is important, too. In a radio play everything has to be expressed using sound, but in a film the director can add visual clues such as facial movements, body language and visual imagery.

In Year 12 English, you are more likely to be asked about the composition of an oral text, its language use and the effect of the words chosen in terms of audience and purpose.

An aside on ... why we are getting you to look at oral text

Remember that even though you may not be assessed using an oral text as the basis of your close reading, the techniques you learn about for oral text are relevant to the study of other text types too, both poetry and prose. You will find examples of clichés, personal pronouns, similes and alliteration; you will see how a writer can create a mood or tone; you will appreciate how an audience is appealed to by careful choice of vocabulary and structure of sentences. It's **all** relevant to **all** types of text.

Listen to, hear, understand ...

ISBN 9780170244213

Terminology you should be confident with ...

In Year 12 it is important to include the technical language of English in your answer. The list below is what we would expect you to know at this level.

You will notice in the left hand margin there are two circles labelled 'I know' and 'I need to check'. Read through the list and tick the box that best describes your knowledge of each literary term. Look up all the ones you don't know in the Language Lists at the end of this book.

I know / I need to check

- ○ ○ **Alliteration**
- ○ ○ **Anecdotes**
- ○ ○ **Clichés**
- ○ ○ **Emotive words**
- ○ ○ **Examples**
- ○ ○ **Figures of speech**
- ○ ○ **Hyperbole**

I know / I need to check

- ○ ○ **Imagery**
- ○ ○ **Imperative**
- ○ ○ **Informal language**
- ○ ○ **Listing**
- ○ ○ **Pause**
- ○ ○ **Personal pronouns**

I know / I need to check

- ○ ○ **References to authority**
- ○ ○ **Repetition**
- ○ ○ **Rhetorical question**
- ○ ○ **Use of humour**
- ○ ○ **Use of statistics**

New to you may be ...

Audience appeal

A good speaker knows their audience before they begins and reads their audience as they speak. A student wanting to be voted onto their school's Board of Trustees will talk about current issues facing students at that school. An aspiring politican wanting to be voted in by a community facing a major issue (e.g., West Coast: logging, Waihi: mining) will talk about that issue above all else.

Allusion/reference

An indirect reference to an event or person.

For example: Martin Luther King's 'Five score years ago ...' alludes to the opening of Lincoln's Gettysburg address and its statement of equality and freedom.

The effect is to extend an image or idea in the listener's mind.

Anaphora

Repetition of a word or phrase in successive clauses.

For example: 'I have a dream.'

'Let freedom ring...' (Martin Luther King)

The effect is often one of emphasis.

ISBN 9780170244213

Antithesis

The contrast between words or ideas. Used to emphasise a difference and/or to give the effect of balance.

For example: 'He knew everything about literature except how to enjoy it.'

(*Catch 22* by Joseph Heller)

'I come to bury Caesar, not to praise him.
The evil that men do lives after them;
The good is oft interred with their bones;'

(Mark Antony in Shakespeare's *Julius Caesar*)

'The love of liberty is the love of others; the love of power is the love of ourselves.'

(William Hazlitt, 19th century journalist)

Parallelism

Comparison or correspondence of two successive passages:

'On the 4th of July we count our blessings, and there are so many to count. We're thankful for the families we love. We're thankful for the opportunities in America. We're thankful for our freedom ...'

(George W. Bush, 4 July 2002)

Did you know that the mathematical sign for equals was invented by someone who said that nothing is more similar or equal than two parallel lines?

Quotations

Sayings that sum up in a nutshell what a speaker wishes to convey are useful devices. Proverbs are particularly useful in this way.

For example: He who hesitates is lost.

Least said, soonest mended.

Where there's a will there's a way.

The hand that rocks the cradle rules the world.

Of course, a well-known phrase is also often a cliché – repeated too often to have much effect. A good speaker or speech-writer will choose his or her words carefully and not rely too much on the 'tried and true'. A quotation can give a speech an air of greater authority. For example quoting from the Bible can suggest that God is on your side. The phrase 'an eye for an eye' comes from Exodus. The phrase 'turn the other cheek' originates from the Bible too – 'whosoever shall smite thee on thy right cheek, turn to him the other also.'

Tricolon

The division of an idea into three harmonious parts, usually of increasing power.

For example: '... government of the people, by the people, for the people'

(Abraham Lincoln, President of the USA, in the Gettysburg Address at the dedication of a graveyard at Gettysburg, one of the battlefields of the American Civil War in 1863.)

'Today, our fellow citizens, our way of life, our very freedom came under attack ...'

(George Bush, President of the USA, in his address to the nation after the terrorist attack on New York, 11 September 2001.)

ISBN 9780170244213

Oral language

To sum up, this chart draws together all of terminology you will use as you close read oral text. Use it as a reference whenever you look at a piece of unfamiliar oral text.

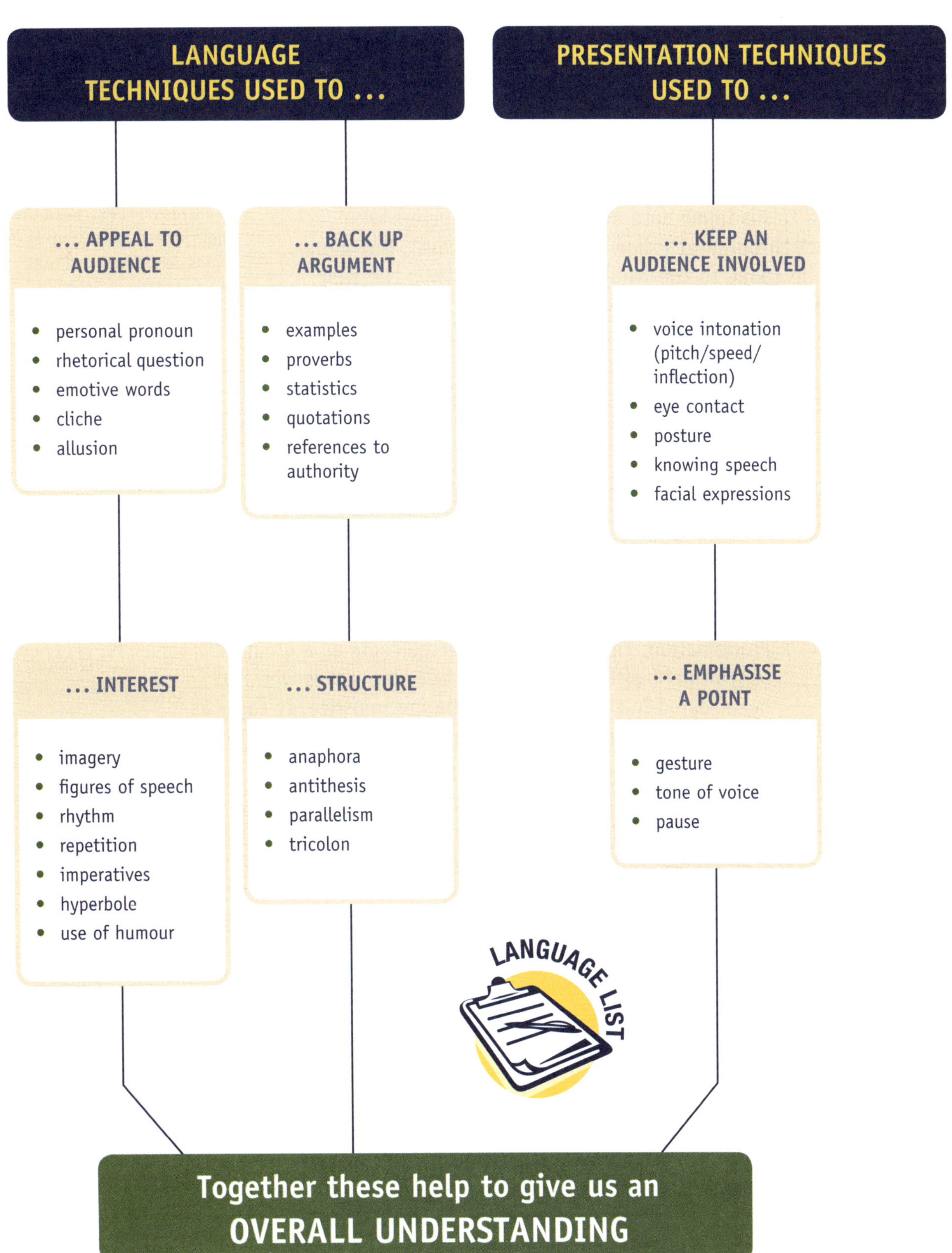

ISBN 9780170244213

Let's have a closer look at an oral text

In order to fully appreciate any great speech it is necessary to know who said/spoke/delivered it, on what occasion, to what purpose, and how it was received. If you have enough time it is worthwhile doing a little research about any speech you are asked to close read.

This oral text is the opening of a speech delivered by Dr Martin Luther King Jr, a prominent civil rights campaigner in mid 20th century US. Two hundred thousand people heard him speak at a march in Washington on 27 August 1963, for 'Jobs and Freedom' on the 100th anniversary of President Abraham Lincoln's signing of the Emancipation Proclamation that freed all slaves in the US.

Dr King spoke to his immediate audience of supporters who applauded him throughout (via a national broadcast). But more significantly he spoke to the whole US nation. It was the first time a speech of this kind had been delivered by an African American through the media in its entirety. It marked a turning point in the history of race relations in the US.

Find out more about the conditions for African American US citizens in 1963. Read the whole speech by Dr King. It begins very calmly and rises to a crescendo of appeal to the audience in the cry and response way that African American gospel preachers reach their congregations.

allusions

alliteration

parallelism

metaphor

antithesis

anaphora

metaphor

emotive language throughout

metaphor

emotive words

I am happy to join with you today in what will go down in history as the greatest demonstration for freedom in the history of our nation.

Five score years ago, a great American, in whose symbolic shadow we stand today, signed the Emancipation Proclamation. This momentous decree came as a great beacon light of hope to millions of Negro slaves who had been seared in the flames of withering injustice. It came as a joyous daybreak to end the long night of their captivity.

But 100 years later, the Negro still is not free. One hundred years later, the life of the Negro is still sadly crippled by the manacles of segregation and the chains of discrimination. One hundred years later, the Negro lives on a lonely island of poverty in the midst of a vast ocean of material prosperity. One hundred years later, the Negro is still languished in the corners of American society and finds himself an exile in his own land. And so we've come here today to dramatize a shameful condition.

In a sense we've come to our nation's capital to cash a check. When the architects of our republic wrote the magnificent words of the Constitution and the Declaration of Independence, they were signing a promissory note to which every American was to fall heir. This note was a promise that all men – yes, black men as well as white men – would be guaranteed the unalienable rights of life, liberty, and the pursuit of happiness.

ISBN 9780170244213

Now look at another part of the speech. Annotate this yourself. Some techniques have been indicated through underlining, but there are others. Be sure to consider their effect. Find and underline each example used in the terminology list. Look for other language techniques like alliteration, use of personal pronouns, light/dark imagery, emotive words, metaphors etc. Remember that words and phrases may be examples of more than one technique.

Let us not wallow in the valley of despair. I say to you today my friends – so even though we face the difficulties of today and tomorrow, I still have a dream. It is a dream deeply rooted in the American dream.

I have a dream that one day this nation will rise up and live out the true meaning of its creed: 'We hold these truths to be self-evident, that all men are created equal.'

I have a dream that one day on the red hills of Georgia the sons of former slaves and the sons of former slave owners will be able to sit down together at the table of brotherhood.

I have a dream that one day even the state of Mississippi, a state sweltering with the heat of injustice, sweltering with the heat of oppression, will be transformed into an oasis of freedom and justice.

I have a dream that my four little children will one day live in a nation where they will not be judged by the color of their skin but by the content of their character.

I have a dream today.

I have a dream that one day down in Alabama, with its vicious racists, with its governor having his lips dripping with the words of interposition and nullification – one day right there in Alabama little black boys and black girls will be able to join hands with little white boys and white girls as sisters and brothers.

I have a dream today.

...

This will be the day, this will be the day when all of God's children will be able to sing with new meaning 'My country 'tis of thee, sweet land of liberty, of thee I sing. Land where my fathers died, land of the Pilgrim's pride, from every mountainside, let freedom ring!' And if America is to be a great nation, this must become true.

...

Let freedom ring. And when this happens, and when we allow freedom to ring – when we let it ring from every village and every hamlet, from every state and every city, we will be able to speed up that day when all of God's children – black men and white men, Jews and Gentiles, Protestants and Catholics – will be able to join hands and sing in the words of the old Negro spiritual: 'Free at last! Free at last! Thank God Almighty, we are free at last!'

ISBN 9780170244213

Oral close reading practice

A variety of prose texts and accompanying close reading questions are provided in this section for you to practise.

Text 1

Read the following passage from the play *St Joan* by G. B. Shaw, about Joan of Arc. Annotate important features (see page 111).

You promised me my life, but you lied. You think that life is nothing but not being stone dead. It is not the bread and water I fear: I can live on bread: when have I asked for more? It is no hardship to drink water if the water be clean. Bread has no sorrow for me, and water no affliction.

But to shut me from the light of the sky and the sight of the fields and flowers; to chain my feet so that I can never again ride with the soldiers nor climb the hills; to make me breathe foul damp darkness, and keep me from everything that brings me back to the love of God when your wickedness and foolishness tempt me to hate Him: all this is worse than the furnace in the Bible that was heated seven times.

I could do without my warhorse; I could drag about in a skirt; I could let the banners and the trumpets and the knights and soldiers pass me and leave me behind as they leave the other women, if only I could still hear the wind in the trees, the larks in the sunshine, the young lambs crying through the healthy frost, and the blessed church bells that send my angel voices floating to me on the wind.

Further information about the historical character Joan of Arc is on the Internet.

Before you go further ...

Complete the following chart.

What is it **about**?	What is the **purpose**?	What is the **tone**?	Who is the **audience**?

ISBN 9780170244213

Answer the following questions in as much detail as possible:

1 Using information from the first paragraph, explain why Joan is so angry.

2 What is the worst thing about being imprisoned for Joan?

3 How does the writer reveal her longing for her former freedom in paragraph 2?

4 Look at the third paragraph. What does it tell you about the things Joan likes? Do you see any anomaly there?

5 Which phrase in the last paragraph suggests that Joan dislikes being female? Why does it suggest this?

6 Imagine this scene being played to an audience. What is the writer trying to get the audience to think about?

ISBN 9780170244213

Text 2

Read the following speech. Annotate important features (see page 111).

I arrive home, my after-school job completed. It is half past six. I've been on the go, classes, lunch-time debate meetings, and work, for 11 hours, it's definitely time for a break. I flop into my favourite chair and turn on the TV. Ahhh, half an hour of comedy – just what I needed.

For half an hour, all my problems are forgotten, as I watch, and laugh with, the characters of *Friends*, along with countless other teenagers around the country. We, as a group, have been entertained – no deep-seated evil has come of this.

There have been no subliminal messages telling me to kill the President, and I feel no need to go and poison the local water supply. Nothing but good has come from my half hour – I am now relaxed, and can continue without blowing up into a million tiny little pieces.

TV's only influence on me has been to make me laugh – surely this cannot be anything but good for me.

Good evening ...

My team ...

Before I continue, my team and I would firstly like to slightly clarify tonight's moot further. We are not here today to argue that watching television is a good way to spend your Sunday afternoons. We are here to discuss whether or not watching the images and listening to the sounds created have positive effects on us. Are we stimulated by them, do we learn, do we explore, do we develop new ways of thinking? The answer is a resounding yes.

The News. One of the most influential programmes on TV today, and it consistently rates among the top three most watched programmes. Now what benefit does watching the news give us? Put simply, it broadens our horizons.

How many of us would have known about the great Buddhist statues blown up in Afghanistan, had it not been for the TV news? How many of us even knew that these wonderful creations existed before they were reported on the news? I can't raise my hand, and it seems that none of you can either. The only way that I found out the US presidential results, arguably the most important election in the world, was through the TV news. I could go on all night, but I've only got eight minutes, so I'd better move on! My point is that, were it not for television, its ease, convenience and relatively low costs, the majority of our population would not have the foggiest about many extraordinarily important international, and national events.

I can almost hear our opposition thinking that newspapers, radio, and other forms of media would take over were it not for TV news – but this is simply not true. TV is too easy, too convenient and too cheap to be replaced. This is not to mention our deaf population – who use the pictures and subtitles (thanks, teletext), to provide these people with a service that they could not get anywhere through any other media.

Another very obvious statement that our opposition is bound to come up with tonight is that television is too violent and our children learn and copy this. How very predictable. What they fail to realise is that we are talking about effects on the home ...

Andrew White

ISBN 9780170244213

Before you go further …

Complete the following chart.

What is it **about**?	What is the **purpose**?	What is the **tone**?	Who is the **audience**?

Answer the following questions in as much detail as possible:

1 Who is the speaker? What is his role in the debating team?

2 What is the occasion?

3 Who is the audience?

4 What is the intention of the speech?

5 What techniques are used to achieve that intention? Look especially for examples of: use of anecdote, colloquial language, hyperbole, rhetorical question, parallelism, humour.

6 Was the intention realised? Was the speech successful? Use the information you have highlighted in the previous examination of the text to write an explanation of your response.

ISBN 9780170244213

Something a little different - POLITICAL SPEECHES

In this final section on oral text we are giving you excerpts from two recent political speeches. There are similarities and differences between them. The questions that follow will ask you to compare and contrast these speeches.

We know, you know it's not just the words that make a fine speech. Speakers need to stand up straight and look the audience in the eye. US President, Barack Obama is very, very good at this – he uses an autocue; watch his gaze range across his audience as he checks his text in the autocues. Those speakers who have to settle for hand-held notes can be a bit more challenged as they have to glance down from time to time. The best speakers know what they want to say and say it; they don't read it. They speak with conviction. They exude confidence.

But the speechwriter has to provide the content of the speech in style too and there are some simple techniques that can be spotted easily.

Speech 1

This is the beginning of Barack Obama's election victory speech, November 2008.

> Hello Chicago. If there is anyone out there who still doubts that America is a place where all things are possible, who still wonders if the dream of our founders is alive in our time, who still questions the power of our democracy, tonight is your answer.

In this opening paragraph, all one single sentence after the greeting, we have the core of good persuasive language.

There's a **TRICOLON:** three parallel phrases building to a conclusion.
Who still doubts ..., wonders ..., questions

There's **REPETITION:** *who still* x3

There's a **RHETORICAL QUESTION:**
If there is ... with the built in answer *tonight is your answer* ...

There's the use of the **INCLUSIVE PERSONAL PRONOUN:** *our time, our democracy*

There's **ALLUSION:** to America's founding document that states all men are equal (Obama is of African American descent and he was elected President ...)

Sometimes it really helps to read the speech aloud to **FEEL** the speech patterns. To **HEAR** it rather than read it is great, too. The Internet can help you do that.

ISBN 9780170244213

Read the rest of Obama's speech. Annotate important features (see page 111).

It's the answer told by lines that stretched around schools and churches in numbers this nation has never seen, by people who waited three hours and four hours, many for the first time in their lives, because they believed that this time must be different, that their voices could be that difference.

It's the answer spoken by young and old, rich and poor, Democrat and Republican, black, white, Hispanic, Asian, Native American, gay, straight, disabled and not disabled; Americans who sent a message to the world that we have never been just a collection of individuals or a collection of red states and blue states; we are, and always will be, the United States of America.

It's the answer that led those who've been told for so long, by so many, to be cynical and fearful and doubtful about what we can achieve, to put their hands on the arc of history and bend it once more toward the hope of a better day. It's been a long time coming, but tonight, because of what we did on this day, in this election, at this defining moment, change has come to America.

...

I was never the likeliest candidate for this office. We didn't start with much money or many endorsements. Our campaign was not hatched in the halls of Washington – it began in the backyards of Des Moines and the living rooms of Concord and the front porches of Charleston.

It was built by working men and women who dug into what little savings they had to give five dollars and ten dollars and twenty dollars to this cause. It grew strength from the young people who rejected the myth of their generation's apathy; who left their homes and their families for jobs that offered little pay and less sleep; from the not-so-young people who braved the bitter cold and scorching heat to knock on the doors of perfect strangers; from the millions of Americans who volunteered, and organised, and proved that more than two centuries later, a government of the people, by the people and for the people has not perished from this Earth. This is your victory.

...

ISBN 9780170244213

Speech 2

This is the beginning of John Key, Prime Minister of New Zealand's speech after the Christchurch earthquake, February 2011. Annotate important features (see page 111).

New Zealanders have woken to a tragedy unfolding in the great city of Christchurch. The earthquake that struck the Canterbury region at ten to one yesterday has wreaked death and destruction on a dreadful scale. There is no reason that can make sense of this event. No words that can spare our pain.

We are witnessing the havoc caused by a violent and ruthless act of nature. Many people have lost their lives. Families have lost cherished loved ones. Mates have lost their mates. These deaths are the greatest loss. They remind us that buildings are just buildings, roads just roads, but our people are irreplaceable.

Today all New Zealanders grieve for you, Christchurch. To all those who woke up in Christchurch today feeling lucky to be alive, we know that you too are shocked, unnerved and grieving. We know that your loss is sharpened by fear. Our minds go to the mothers and fathers comforting children struck by anxiety and disbelief. They go to the elderly, infirm and isolated who experienced this event alone and who remain blunted by shock. And they go to each and every Cantabrian who has stoically endured six months of aftershocks, only to be hit by the biggest shock of all.

On behalf of all New Zealand let me say to all of you: we feel your pain, as only a small nation can, for none of us feel removed from this event. I am a proud son of Christchurch. I was raised there, I got my first job there, my sister lives there, my mother died there, I know what a wonderful place it is.

But my connection to Christchurch is no rare thing. All New Zealanders have a piece of our heart in Christchurch. All our lives are touched by this event. A friend or family member who lives there. A time spent studying there or a memorable experience had there. We feel connected to your suffering. Your tragedy is our tragedy.

Today I want Christchurch to hear this message: you will get through this. This proud country is right behind you and we are backing you with all our might.

The world is with us. Our Australian neighbours, our British and American friends, the great countries of this world, all are putting their shoulder to your wheel. They are sending their support, their expertise, their people to help us.

Christchurch, today is the day your great comeback begins. Though your buildings are broken, your streets awash, and your hearts are aching, your great spirit will overcome.

...

ISBN 9780170244213

These questions are asking you to compare the speeches. Answer them in as much detail as possible.

You can find the entire texts of both these speeches on the Internet.

1 What similarities and differences can you see between these two speakers, audiences, occasions?

2 What is the purpose of each speech?

3 How does each speaker involve his personal life in the speech?

4 How does each speaker involve his audience in his speech?

ISBN 9780170244213

5 Choose three techniques and say how each has been used in each speech. Look for similarities or differences. Do not repeat material from previous answers.

Technique 1

Technique 2

Technique 3

6 Are these successful speeches? Explain why you agree or disagree with reference to and quotations from the texts.

ISBN 9780170244213

Compare ... Contrast ... Connect

'No man is an island' the famous poet John Donne wrote 400 hundred years ago. It's true.

Our lives are a series of **connections** – with family, with friends, with schoolmates, teachers, colleagues at work and at play. It's the same with our language and literature. What we read, write, listen to and watch is all **connected** in some way to our own lives and to each other.

At Year 12 in your study of English you will be asked to look for **connections**. We started this approach to passages in ***Achievement English @ Year 11*** and here we will continue to ask you to analyse a group of passages which **connect**. We will suggest ways to read a group of texts rather than look at a single text in isolation.

You may be asked to look for **connections** in a set of unfamiliar short texts or a group of longer texts that you choose for yourself. This work will help you to prepare for such a task. You will use the same techniques, the same skills you have developed for studying a single text. Perhaps the three most important words will be **compare**, **contrast** and **connect**.

COMPARE	CONTRAST	CONNECT
Emphasise **similarities** and mention differences.	Compare by showing **differences.**	**Link together** related elements.

So, let's think about what might be similar, what might connect the texts:

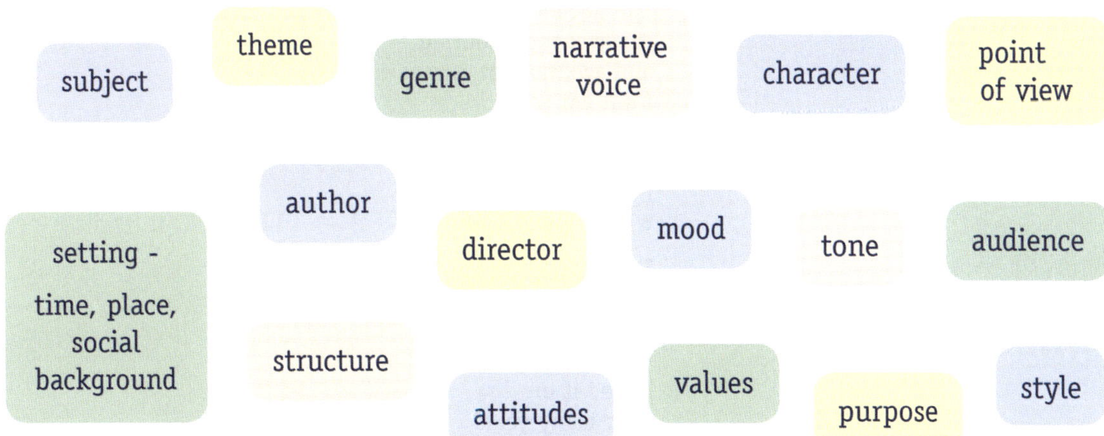

These are not new words, are they? We repeat, you will be using the same ways to analyse these texts as all the others you have studied in the past; it's just that the focus will be different.

ISBN 9780170244213

Here are four texts. Each one stands alone on its own merit, but there are connections to be made between them, too.

Text 1

Read the following poem carefully. Annotate important features (see pages 65-71).

My Mother's Coat

As a child
I felt protected and warm
Wrapped
in my mother's coat
It must have looked funny
Big brown eyes
Peering from its folds
As if that was all there was
to me

I remember
Its unique threads
Unusual and coarse
Their slenderness
belied their strength
Its tivaevae-like panels
of thin fabric
An effective shield
against bitter winters
The colours loud
Shouting for attention
and space

My mother always wore
her coat with pride
Unfazed
by its highlighter effect
Marking her out
In a Papaa crowd
But blending beautifully
At every putuputuanga

I remember too
With youthful disdain
Discarding my mother's coat
Not for me
The uncool design
extravagant colouring
and awkward fit
I did not want
to be marked
If only
I knew then
What I know now

She wears it still
Her brooch of pride
brilliant and bright
And not long ago
I tried it on
after many years
Although it's not really me
It's because of her
I can sew
my own

Ta'i George

Ta'i was born in Otara, Auckland to Cook Island parents

ISBN 9780170244213

Before you go further ...

Complete the following chart.

What is it **about**?	What is the **purpose**?	What is the **tone**?	Who is the **audience**?

Answer the following questions in as much detail as possible:

1 What does the coat represent to the narrator?

2 When she was a child how did the coat help her?

3 What does the narrator feel the coat shows about her mother?

4 Explain the phrase 'awkward fit'.

5 Why does the writer use alliteration in verse 3?

6 Explain the double meaning in the words 'I can sew my own'.

7 Explain what the writer is saying about her Cook Island heritage and especially the development of her relationship with her mother in this poem. Can you relate these feelings to your own or a friend's life?

ISBN 9780170244213

Text 2

Read the following passage carefully. It is from a regular newspaper columnist. Annotate important features (see page 11 and/or 36).

Words highlighted in blue are those you may need to check the meaning of.
Words highlighted in yellow draw your attention to things you need to notice.
Answer the questions using your personal annotations.

Extract from: *There's much to learn from Tiger Mothers*

One of my children once accused me of being just like an Asian parent. I took it as a compliment.

These 2 words suggest what?

I used to think of myself as a strict, demanding mother, but after reading the Yale professor Amy Chua's *Wall Street Journal* article on 'why Chinese mothers are superior', excerpted from her book *Battle Hymn of the Tiger Mother*, I now realise what an underachieving pushover I've been.

Look up this allusion.

Can you see the pun?

I failed as a Tiger Mum. I was far too easy on my children. I gave them choices. No wonder my children didn't become competition-winning pianists or violinists.

Literary technique? Used for?

As Chua writes: 'A lot of people wonder how Chinese parents raise such stereotypically successful kids. They wonder what these parents do to produce so many math whizzes and music prodigies, what it's like inside the family, and whether they could do it too. Well, I can tell them, because I've done it.'

We may be sincere about wanting our children to be kind caring citizens above all else, but what parent hasn't harboured dreams of raising the next musical child prodigy or maths whizz?

Literary technique? Used for?

Yet Chua's recipe for success can be a little hard to swallow. Her two (now teenaged) daughters weren't permitted to waste their time on sleepovers, playdates or taking part in school plays. Watching TV and playing computer games were out of the question, as was refusing to learn the violin or piano. And getting anything less than an A, or failing to be the number one student in every class except gym and drama weren't tolerated.

Literary technique? Means?

Such was Chua's uncompromising commitment to the advancement of her children that she once refused to let her then 7-year-old daughter have water or a toilet break until she'd mastered a difficult musical piece, even threatening to burn all her stuffed animals when she rebelled. She didn't pretend to like the substandard birthday cards her daughters gave her either; she demanded new ones.

Chua thinks Western parents worry too much about self-esteem – she called her daughter 'garbage' when she got

ISBN 9780170244213

cheeky – and scoffs at the idea that a child's happiness should be a primary consideration. Happiness comes with mastery, and mastery comes with practice, practice, practice.

...

The results seem to be on Chua's side. Her daughters get straight As and win music competitions; she says they're happy and well-adjusted, so who are we to judge?

New York Times columnist David Brooks argues that Chua 'is the logical extension of the prevailing elite practices. She does everything over-pressurising upper-middle-class parents are doing. She's just hard core'.

As Chua says, you don't have to be Chinese to be a Chinese mother.

What does this mean?

...

The author ends her article like this:

Still, there's much we could learn from the Tiger Mothers – not the least the belief that intelligence and ability aren't innate or the preserve of the lucky few, but in fact skills which can be developed in any child with the right encouragement and support, and a lot of hard work.

Tapu Misa

Before you go further ...

Complete the following chart.

What is it **about**?	What is the **purpose**?	What is the **tone**?	Who is the **audience**?

Answer these questions in as much detail as possible:

1 This is an opinion piece from a newspaper. Does Tapu Misa recommend 'Chinese mother' upbringing for children?

ISBN 9780170244213

Text 3

Read the following extract carefully. It is from *Romeo and Juliet* by William Shakespeare. The play was written over 400 years ago, so it is possible you will need to look up several words. Annotate the important features.

Words highlighted in blue are those you may need to check the meaning of.
Words highlighted in yellow draw your attention to things you need to notice.
Answer the questions using your personal annotations.

Context: Capulet has informed his daughter Juliet that he has arranged a marriage for her with a nobleman called Paris. However, Juliet has fallen in love with Romeo and has secretly married him instead. Her father reacts to her disobedience.

CAPULET
Soft! Take me with you,
take me with you wife.
How! Will she none?
Doth she not give us thanks?
Is she not proud? Doth she not count her blest,
Unworthy as she is, that we have wrought
So worthy a gentleman to be her bridegroom?

JULIET
Not proud, you have; but thankful you have:
Proud can I never be of what I hate;
But thankful even for hate, that is meant love.

CAPULET
How now, how now, chop-logic! What is this?
'Proud,' and 'I thank you,' and 'I thank you not;'
And yet 'not proud,' mistress minion, you,
Thank me no thankings, nor, proud me no prouds,
But fettle your fine joints 'gainst Thursday next,
To go with Paris to Saint Peter's Church,
Or I will drag thee on a hurdle thither.
Out, you green-sickness carrion! Out, you baggage!
You tallow-face!

LADY CAPULET
Fie, fie! What are you mad?

ISBN 9780170244213

JULIET
Good father, I beseech you on my knees,
Hear me with patience but to speak a word.

CAPULET
Hang thee young baggage! Disobedient wretch!
I tell thee what: get thee to church o' Thursday,
Or never after look me in the face:
Speak not, reply not, do not answer me;
My fingers itch. Wife, we scarce thought us blest
That God had lent us but this only child;
But now I see this one is one too much,
And that we have a curse in having her.
Out on her, hilding!

NURSE
God in heaven bless her!
You are to blame, my lord, to rate her so...
...

CAPULET
God's bread! It makes me mad:
Day, night, hour, tide, time, work, play,
Alone, in company, still my care hath been
To have her match'd: and having now provided
A gentleman of noble parentage,
Of fair desmesnes, youthful, and nobly train'd,
Stuffed, as they say, with honourable parts,
Proportion'd as one's thought would wish a man;
And then to have a wretched puling fool,
A whining mammet, in her fortune's tender,
To answer "I'll not wed, I cannot love,
I am too young; I pray you, pardon me."
But, as you will not wed, I'll pardon you:
Graze where you will you shall not house with me:
Look to't, think on't, I do not use to jest.
Thursday is near; lay hand on heart, advise:
An you be mine, I'll give you to my friend;
And you be not, hang, beg, starve, die in the streets,
For, by my soul, I'll ne'er acknowledge thee,
Not what is mine shall never do thee good:
Trust to't, bethink you; I'll not be forsworn.
Exit

ISBN 9780170244213

Before you go further ...

Complete the following chart.

What is it **about**?	What is the **purpose**?	What is the **tone**?	Who is the **audience**?

Answer the following questions in as much detail as possible:

1 What is making Capulet so angry?

2 What is his solution to the problem?

3 How does Shakespeare suggest Capulet is wrong?

ISBN 9780170244213

Text 4

Read the following passage carefully. It is an extract from a novel, the fictional diary of a famous New Zealand athlete, Jack Lovelock. Annotate important features (see page 11 and/or 36).

Words highlighted in blue are those you may need to check the meaning of.

Answer the questions using your personal annotations.

Lovelock

The first time I saw a pony, I chased it. This was later, on a wild plain, when we came to live in the mountains. I remember the pony's tail floating in the wind, thinking to myself as I ran after it, that tail is perfect. Why can't I run like that? Afterwards when I told my father about chasing the pony all he said was, 'Did you catch it?'

'No,' I said. 'I wasn't fast enough.'

I was seven or eight at the time. I ran my first race proper when I was ten, at a Boy Scouts' camp. It was a mile and I won by 5 yards. My father was pleased but not as pleased as all that. 'If you'd trained a bit harder,' he said, 'you could have won by 50 yards.' I was sick after that race. I was in bed for two days, vomiting. 'You'll have to do better than this, Jack-o', I told myself, if you're going to please your father. I never did. My father died when I was thirteen, in my first year at boarding school.

At boarding school I borrowed a stop-watch and began to train in secret, like Nurmi. Nurmi was my first hero. One day I read in a newspaper that in Paris, France, Paavo Nurmi has won three Gold Medals and broken three world records in the space of a single day, two of them in the space of an hour. I decided that if I could grow up to win an Olympic medal like Nurmi, that would please my father. The last race I ran before my father died was in the school steeplechase, although I must still have been a junior. It was run over the golf course. Halfway round the course, I was so far in front that I knew I would break the record. Then someone called out that I had missed a marker and I had to go back. By the time I had run back and gone round the marker, I had lost 200 yards and the field was in front of me. I set off after them. I caught the front-runner and passed him just before the tape was reached. I won. But I hadn't broken the record.

'What happened?' my father asked.

'I missed a marker. I missed a marker and had to go back.'

'You made a mistake, Jack.'

'But I missed a marker, Dad!'

It was no use. I could tell by the expression in his eyes, a sort of blankness that came over them, that he was disappointed in me. My father had absolute standards – not just in running but in everything. Yet it was the running that seemed to matter most, even though running was not in his blood. Or mine. My father was employed by a mining company. My mother is a piano teacher. There is nothing in the family to account for me. I have probably made my father sound a bit of an ogre, but, strangely enough, as I grew older I came to agree with him and adopt his standards. At school in my final year I won so many honours the Rector took the unusual step of announcing to all the parents that I would one day win a Rhodes – as indeed a few years later I did. My father would have wept to hear the Rector say that. My father taught me. I feared him, and have remained grateful to him. He taught me to strive. To do the right thing. I don't mean by that that he still haunts me, and yet there always seems to be someone watching at my elbow or looking over my shoulder, like this morning. This morning's interview is a good example. It has always been like this. Every time I manage to come alight, to catch fire or lose my inhibitions, just at the point when I am reaching out to grasp the pony's tail, I seem to make a mistake and come down with a thump. Something always happens to spoil the vision.

James McNeish

Before you go further ...

Complete the following chart.

What is it **about**?	What is the **purpose**?	What is the **tone**?	Who is the **audience**?

Answer the following questions in as much detail as possible:

1 What does Jack remember most about the way his father treated him?

2 Does Jack think his father was/is a positive influence? Do you?

ISBN 9780170244213

Making connections

Now it is time to look at this group of texts to see any connections between them. Refer to at least three of the texts as you answer these questions:

You might use the grids you have filled in to help you form a basis for your answers using the similarities and differences in:

- Content: the subject of each text.
- Audience: for whom the writer is writing.
- Style: vocabulary, nouns and verbs; descriptive words like adjectives and adverbs; figures of speech; facts; emotive words...
- Purpose: theme/s, ideas, opinions, intentions...

1 What connections in time and place can you see in these texts?

2 Describe any similarities or differences you can see in the way the themes are presented.

3 Do any of the writers have similar opinions? Do any of these writers have different opinions?

ISBN 9780170244213

On your own ... again

Now that you have worked though our example it is time for you to have a go on your own. Remember to apply everything you have learnt in the previous sections.

Carefully read the instructions first so that you are aware of exactly what you need to do.

Take each text in turn and:

- Read it through once for understanding.
- Read it through again circling, underlining, linking ideas etc as you go.
- Look at the specific questions on the text and answer them.

We think you will find it easy to spot the connection/s between these texts.

Text 1

Read the following poem carefully. Carew was writing in the early 17th century. Poems were often written to celebrate beauty. Annotate important features (See pages 65-71).

The True Beauty

He that loves a rosy cheek
Or a coral lip admires
Or from starlike eyes doth seek
Fuel to maintain his fires
As old Time makes these decay,
So his flames must waste away.

But a smooth and steadfast mind,
Gentle thoughts, and calm desires,
Hearts with equal love combined,
Kindle never-dying fires:-
Where these are not, I despise
Lovely cheeks or lips or eyes.

Thomas Carew

ISBN 9780170244213

Before you go further ...

Complete the following chart.

What is it **about**?	What is the **purpose**?	What is the **tone**?	Who is the **audience**?

Answer the following questions in as much detail as possible. Use quotations and references to the text to support your ideas.

1 What are the first three images? Why are they important?

2 What ideal does alliteration draw your attention to in verse 2?

3 In lines 1-4 and 7-9 Carew compares female attributes. Explain his preferences.

4 Comment on the structure of this poem.

5 Do you agree with the idea expressed in this poem?

ISBN 9780170244213

Text 2

Read the following passage carefully. It is an extract from Shakespeare's play, *Romeo and Juliet*. Here Juliet is waiting for her new, secretly-married husband, Romeo. Annotate important features.

JULIET
Come, civil night,
Thou sober-suited matron, all in black,
And learn me how to lose a winning match,
Play'd for a pair of stainless maidenhoods.
Hood my unmann'd blood, bating in my cheeks,
With thy black mantle, till strange love grow bold,
Think true love acted simple modesty.
Come, night, come, Romeo, come, thou day in night;
For thou wilt lie upon the wings of night
Whiter than new snow on a raven's back.
Come, gentle night, come, loving, black-brow'd night,
Give me my Romeo; and, when he shall die,
Take him and cut him out in little stars,
And he will make the face of heaven so fine
That all the world will be in love with night
And pay no worship to the garish sun.

Act 3, Scene 2, lines 10-25

Before you go further ...

Complete the following chart.

What is it **about**?	What is the **purpose**?	What is the **tone**?	Who is the **audience**?

ISBN 9780170244213

Answer the following questions in as much detail as possible. Use quotations and references to the text to support your ideas.

1 List the images that are used to describe the loved one. What are the similarities between these images?

2 What idea does Shakespeare convey through the image 'new snow on a raven's back'? How is this theme extended through other images in the poem?

3 How is night introduced? Does it seem welcomed or feared? Consider the words Shakespeare links with it.

4 What is Juliet's death wish for Romeo?

5 Underline all the long vowels in lines 17-20 and explain their effect.

6 Why is 'come night' repeated?

7 Note where alliteration is used. What idea or image is Shakespeare drawing attention to by using alliteration?

ISBN 9780170244213

Text 3

Read the following passage carefully. It is an an extract from *Persuasion*, a novel by Jane Austen. Annotate important features.

... Captain Frederick Wentworth ... was, at that time, a remarkably fine young man, with a great deal of intelligence, spirit and brilliancy; and Anne an extremely pretty girl, with gentleness, modesty, taste, and feeling. Half the sum of attraction, on either side, might have been enough, for he had nothing to do, and she had hardly any body to love; but the encounter of such lavish recommendations could not fail. They were gradually acquainted, and when acquainted, rapidly and deeply in love. It would be difficult to say which had seen highest perfection in the other, or which had been the happiest; she, in receiving his declarations and proposals, or he in having them accepted.

A short period of exquisite felicity followed, and but a short one. Troubles soon arose. Sir Walter, on being applied to, without actually withholding his consent, or saying it should never be, gave it all the negative of great astonishment, great coldness, great silence, and a professed resolution of doing nothing for his daughter. He thought it a very degrading alliance; and Lady Russell, though with more tempered and pardonable pride, received it as a most unfortunate one.

Anne Elliot, with all her claims of birth, beauty, and mind, to throw herself away at nineteen – involve herself at nineteen in an engagement with a young man, who had nothing but himself to recommend him, and no hopes of attaining affluence but in the chances of a most uncertain profession, and no connexions to secure even his farther rise in that profession – would be, indeed, a throwing away, which she grieved to think of! Anne Elliot, so young; known to so few, to be snatched off by a stranger without alliance or fortune; or rather sunk by him into a state of most wearing, anxious, youth-killing dependance! It must not be, if by any fair interference of friendship, any representations from one who had almost a mother's love, and mother's rights, it would be prevented.

(Anne is persuaded to refuse Captain Wentworth, but no-one takes his place for her)

... but Anne, at seven-and-twenty, thought very differently from what she had been made to think at nineteen. She did not blame Lady Russell, she did not blame herself for having been guided by her; but she felt that were any young person in similar circumstances to apply to her for counsel, they would never receive any of such certain immediate wretchedness, such uncertain future good ...

How eloquent could Anne Elliot have been! how eloquent, at least, were her wishes on the side of early warm attachment, and a cheerful confidence in futurity, against that over-anxious caution which seems to insult exertion and distrust Providence! She had been forced into prudence in her youth, she learned romance as she grew older: the natural sequel of an unnatural beginning.

ISBN 9780170244213

Before you go further ...

Complete the following chart.

What is it **about**?	What is the **purpose**?	What is the **tone**?	Who is the **audience**?

Answer the following questions in as much detail as possible. Use quotations and references to the text to support your ideas.

1 What is the narrative voice? How does this affect your understanding?

2 Why are Wentworth and Anne attracted to each other? What comment does the writer make?

3 What do Anne's father and Lady Russell think of the match?

4 Does Anne feel she did the right thing? How do you know?

5 What do you think is the writer's attitude to this influence on Anne?

ISBN 9780170244213

Text 4

Read the following poem carefully. It is written by New Zealander Hone Tuwhare. Annotate important features (see pages 65-71).

Mad

I'm too early.
I wait the long slow minutes out,
my breath inheld, ready
to balloon up into a high, but for the slow
exhalation of my excitement as you turn
into the magic avenue of trees – your hand
held out to me – your hand

to my multiple infarctions –
awarenesses
of coin-silver leaves turning a-squint in air,
muffled footfalls on the footpath;
your naked ankles twinkling in the autumn light.
I close the distance between us
as quickly

as fog does boiling in
from the inner harbour inexorably
as the thunder and beat of train wheels
flashing past a tiny country station just
standing there aghast and quite
inexplicably shaken and lost and
without say.

Well, that is how you infect me: mad ay?

Hone Tuwhare

ISBN 9780170244213

Before you go further ...

Complete the following chart.

What is it **about**?	What is the **purpose**?	What is the **tone**?	Who is the **audience**?

Answer the following questions in as much detail as possible. Use quotations and references to the text to support your ideas.

1 Why does the poet compare himself to a balloon in stanza 1?

2 'Exhalation of my excitement' is which poetic technique? What moment is the poet describing?

3 'Your hand' is repeated. What effect does this create?

4 The poet is bringing out the magic of love when he says 'of coin-silver leaves ... autumn light'. What poetic techniques does he use to do this? Consider the images, alliteration and diction.

5 Why has the poet compared his movement to 'the thunder and beat of train wheels/flashing past a tiny country station'?

6 Comment on the final two words of the poem.

ISBN 9780170244213

Making connections

There is a final question here that requires you to read 'across the text' i.e. which means to pull information from several texts. You will need to:

- Go back to each text and skim read until you get to a place that has relevant information.
- Read this part (and a little before and a little after).
- Stop and think about how this connects to the other passages. Note any ideas you have on the side of the text.
- Do the same for each passage. However be aware that you don't necessarily need to use information from all the texts, perhaps just two are sufficient for that part of your response.
- Using the notes you have jotted down, answer the question in the space provided, making sure that you clearly reference the text and draw conclusions in your answer.

1 Select at least three of these texts and explain the connections you can see between them. You may write about just one or several connections that you can identify.

Remember to support your ideas with quotations and references to the texts where appropriate. And also remember, your personal opinions and responses to these texts count.

Suggestions:
Variations on a theme?
Narrative voices?
Author's sex?
Relevance to social mores of the time (you could look up when each writer was writing).
A timeless human condition?

ISBN 9780170244213

Connections Across Texts

At this point it is useful to look at Achievement Standard 2.7 that requires a similar approach.

In this case you will need to read, watch and listen to at least four texts you have chosen yourself and present the various aspects that link or connect the texts in a written, visual and/or oral form.

> *If you are allowed to choose your own texts for this Standard this is a wonderful opportunity to read what you want to read, to follow your own interests.*

Convincingly analyse significant connections across texts means making reasoned points that develop understandings about the connection(s) being addressed. The aim is to offer some insight or originality in thought or interpretation. It may include explaining how significant aspects shared by each text communicate ideas about contexts, such as human experience, society or the wider world.

As this is an internal assessment your classroom teacher will have his or her own way of approaching the Standard, so we cannot tell you *exactly* how it will work for you, but we can help all the same. It is likely that you will have some texts you have studied in class to springboard from. It will be your job to come up with other texts that are also based on the connection you are establishing.

What you are asked to do

- You will need to select some of the texts yourself.
- You should include a range of texts (i.e. written, visual or oral).
- You are likely to need to include at least four texts.
- They can be short or extended texts but it is probably best to aim for a mixture of the two.
- Select texts you actually like ... you are more likely to be motivated and understand them if you like them!

Using a range of texts

We have already noted that you will need to include a range of texts:

novel, novella, short story, biography, autobiography, children's storybook, poem, lyrics, play, screenplay, blog, non-fiction piece from magazine or newspaper or website.

ISBN 9780170244213

Choosing your texts

Your teacher will most likely give you some guidance on this. In fact it is likely that you will be able to use some of the texts you have studied in class.

At this stage don't limit yourself to only three or four texts. This is the 'brainstorm' stage. Have as many as you can so that you can play with the connections between them.

- Start with at least one text that you have studied in class. Why? Because you know it well, you have already formed opinions, have notes, developed essays etc.

- Look at all the other texts you have studied in class and see if you can pull something else from your year's work. It could be a film, a poem or an extract from a close reading.

- Look at other books or poems these authors have written.

- Look at the books you have read personally. Do any of these fit with those texts you have already chosen?

- Think of films that you have both studied and seen outside of school.

- Think of texts you have studied in previous years. Would any of these fit?

- Think of texts you have heard your peers have studied. Would any of these fit?

- Talk to your teacher.

- Talk to your librarian (both school and local public library).

- Talk to your parents.

- Talk to your friends.

ISBN 9780170244213

Let's look at one student's method of selecting texts

Below is a grid that a student created for texts he considered using. He discovered from his theme column, that he had several texts to use that made a connection with the theme of power being a corrupting influence.

Text	Text type	Genre	Subject	Theme	Date written	Setting
Macbeth Shakespeare	Play UK	Historical drama	Murder of king	Power corrupts	Late 1500s	Scotland, castles, medieval
Of Mice and Men John Steinbeck	Novel US	Drama	Two drifters seek a home	American dream fails	1040s??	California, 1930s
Animal Farm George Orwell	Novel UK	Political satire	Animals rule themselves	Power corrupts	1940s	Imagined future
The God Boy Ian Cross	Novel NZ	Family drama	Religion, tragedy	Effect of upbringing	1950s	NZ 1950s
And still I rise Maya Angelou	Poem, US	Historical?	Treatment of slaves. Attitudes of slaves.	Racial prejudice Corruption	1978	US, (southern states)
The Shawshank Redemption Frank Darabont	Film US	Drama	Unjust imprisonment	Freedom/ Justice/ Corruption Hope	1994	US
To Kill a Mockingbird Harper Lee	Novel/film US	law	Man accused of murder	Racial prejudice	??	US
Bliss Katherine Mansfield	Short story NZ	romance	Woman discovers husband unfaithful	Emotional distress	1920s	NZ 1920s
Strictly Ballroom Baz Luhrmann	Film Aus	Light romance	Dancing competiton	Power corrupts	1990s	Oz 1980s

ISBN 9780170244213

You might create a chart for your own texts on the grid below.

Text	Text type	Genre	Subject	Theme	Date written	Setting

ISBN 9780170244213

An alternative process

People work in different ways. Here's an alternative process.

- Choose your texts (prose, poetry or drama) and ask yourself if there is another text by the same writer to make an extended comparison with.
- Explore other useful texts by the same writer (perhaps non-literary texts such as letters).
- Consider other texts of a similar genre (both contemporary and from other periods).
- Concentrate on only one theme and plan out all the connections that you think it would be useful to make. Use headings such as genre, subject matter, tone, context and style, and develop a clear idea of why each link might be useful.

Getting started

Choose your first text

Reasons for your choice might be:

- You studied the text in class
- You have useful notes on the text
- You enjoyed the text
- You understand the text well
- You can see its theme/s clearly
- You think it is well written
- You like the subject matter
- You relate to the theme
- You ________
- You ________

Choose the other texts

Reasons for your choice might be:

- It's written by the same writer
- It's of the same genre
- It's about the same sort of people
- It's set at the same place
- It's got the same or a similar theme
- It's written in a similar style
- It's about the same subject
- It's ________

Other things to consider

Additional useful information to research might be:

- A writer or director's biographical details
- A period's politics or social history
- A time or place's attitudes or values
- Critics' approaches to the texts
- Reviews of the text

And then

Do what you always do:

- Read, think, plan and prepare before you write.
- Will you write about each text separately or intermingle your references to them? The second way is more sophisticated, but definitely more difficult to manage!
- Each class will have its own requirements for presenting this work so pay close attention to your teacher's instructions about how you are to produce your ideas on the way your texts compare, contrast and connect.

ISBN 9780170244213

What might create a connection?

Think about the usual things you study: subject, character, setting, theme. There will be lots of other possibilities and ways to make connections across different texts. You might choose to look at:

SUBJECT

- surfing
- motorbikes
- horses
- fashion
- rugby
- mountaineering
- music
- aeroplanes
- soccer
- fishing
- politics
- social networking
- exploration
- dance
- theatre
- parents
- computers
- school

CHARACTER

- a teenage girl as the central character, or an elderly male, or a young child, or a young man
  - a daughter
  - a mother
  - a grandfather
- a life story, or a particular time in a person's life like school days or holiday time

THEME

- friendship
- loyalty
- family
- hope
- courage
- fear
- conflict
- love
- ambition
- growing up
- prejudice
- greed
- ambition

GENRE

- thriller
- horror
- gothic
- science fiction
- romance
- chic-lit
- adventure
- historical fiction
- survival stories

NARRATIVE STYLE

- first person narrator
- third person eye-of-god (author tells what every character thinks and feels as well as does and says)
- third person from just one character's perspective

SETTING

TIME

- a historical period:
  - colonial New Zealand
  - Tudor England
  - ancient Rome
- the future
- wartime
- during or just after a disaster

PLACE

- a specific location:
  - Christchurch
  - London
  - Wellington
  - Australia
  - South Africa
- or a general location:
  - in the bush
  - mountains
  - the beach
  - a city
  - the country
  - small town life
  - a new place

SOCIAL BACKGROUND

- poverty
- wealth
- class differences (upstairs/downstairs)
- male/female
- racial grouping
  - African American
  - Maori
  - Pacific Island
  - indigenous peoples
  - Scottish migrants
  - displaced people

ISBN 9780170244213

Presenting your findings

Your teacher will give you the presentation style required for your class. It is most likely to be a written or an oral report (or a combination of the two). It is important to follow the requirements in terms of style and length of piece/time for delivery but here are some thoughts:

Structuring an essay

Think about the best way for you to order your ideas. You might:

- Write in full about each text and then draw a conclusion. This is the most straightforward approach but not so very good for drawing clear comparisons between texts.
- Take the topic of your comparison and deal with each text under that heading/ paragraph. For example if you are comparing or contrasting the various texts' attitude to 'romantic love' write about each one under an introductory sentence. Remember, you will need a concluding sentence too.
- If you have a lot to say on one topic you might break the section into two or more paragraphs, introduce your idea and conclude with your personal opinion in separate paragraphs.
- All the rules about writing an essay – introduction, conclusion, linking paragraphs etc are valid here too.
- If you use quotations from poetry remember to use the line break properly. If your quotation is over two lines, use a forward slash as the line break to show where the end of the first line falls. For example:

  'He has no girl to run her fingers through/His sandy hair'.

  If the quotation is two complete lines or longer, then indent the lines as a quotation within your writing. For example:

  The poet describes the farmhand's loneliness by showing what he does not have:

  'He has no girl to run her fingers through
His sandy hair, and giggle at his side
When Sunday couples walk.'

  Here we see what simple pleasures he notices other young men, who do have a girlfriend, enjoy.

  Notice that the inverted commas are not repeated on each line. Use them just at the beginning and end of the quotation.
- The main aim is to make it easy for your reader to follow your ideas.

Remember this is an English assignment and you are expected to use the language skills you have learnt in English to examine the texts you choose.

ISBN 9780170244213

Guidelines for oral presentations

You may be asked to use your research as the basis for an oral presentation. There is little difference between writing an essay and writing the basis of your presentation. However in most cases you will use PowerPoint to help you illustrate your presentation. Here are some guidelines to help you use this valuable tool effectively.

- Choose the background colour of your slides carefully. A dark background and light font work the best.
- If you have text on your slide choose a font that's easy to read. Arial, Tahoma or Trebuchet are usually recommended.
- Use bullet points so that you use as few words as possible.
- Look at your audience, not at your PowerPoint, when you speak. Eye contact is important.
- Stand on the right side of the projector – we tend to look at the screen from left to right and if you are standing where the eye begins you are a bit of a distraction yourself.
- Use as few slides as possible: less is more.
- Give your audience a moment to digest what is on each slide when you open it.
- Use gesture to direct audience attention to what you want them to notice.
- Keep your body half turned to the audience, even when gesturing or pointing to a slide.
- Say things that link the slides together, e.g. "Now, let's look at…"
- Stand away from the light from the projector!
- Make sure the equipment is working before the audience arrives.

Remember … PowerPoint doesn't communicate – you do!

ISBN 9780170244213

11

Understanding Texts

You have been writing essays to express your response to what you read, watch, listen to or view in your English classroom 'forever' (your word, not ours!) but certainly for several years. So by now you have a grasp of the basic way to write an essay.

You probably can write a straightforward ...

- introduction
- statement, explanation, example x3
- conclusion
- 250 word essay

... very easily by now.

But if you want to revise how to write an essay check out pages 113–121 in **Achievement English @ Year 11**).

So what will be different this time?

- Texts will be more sophisticated.
- Your essays will require more words (at least 350 as a guideline).
- You must convincingly support any statement you make.
- You must offer quotations from the texts accurately.
- Any references to the text must be relevant and accurate.
- You response will probably need to involve your personal opinions.
- Your vocabulary should be comfortably technical.
- Your writing will need to be very accurate in spelling and grammar.

Which text is which?

You will be asked to respond to a written and/or a visual/oral text. This can be confusing as a play is meant to be seen and heard not read, but understanding a Shakespeare play if you don't study the written words beforehand is very tricky. And a novel to be read may be created very differently to a film version of the same story, which is meant to be seen and heard.

Nevertheless, we tend to separate the texts into these categories:

WRITTEN TEXT		VISUAL/ORAL TEXT	
• novel • non-fiction • print media • drama • short story	• poetry/song lyric • digital/online texts • a combination of the above (inter-textual studies)	• film • television programme • radio programme • drama production • graphic novel	• oral performance • a combination of the above (inter-textual studies)

Your classroom teacher is likely to select the texts you study as a class but you may have leeway to select some texts for yourself.

ISBN 9780170244213

Common essay weaknesses

One way of looking at this is to understand what might go wrong for students.

PROBLEM	HOW DOES IT SHOW?	WHAT TO DO?
Student does not know the text	Names spelt incorrectly. Plot elements incorrectly summarised. Names incorrect. Theme incompletely understood. Vague sentences. Other people's words copied badly. Essay does not really fit the question.	Read the text with brain switched on. Think about it. Read it again. Annotate it. THINK! Answer the question.
Student does not understand the text well	Spends most of the essay retelling the plot.	See box above. It's important to write about a text you understand. You cannot understand a text fully if you don't read it carefully and think about what the author is trying to say to you.
Student seems incapable of good written English	Incomprehensible handwriting. Spelling mistakes; sentence construction errors; lack of paragraphing.	Give yourself enough time to write with care. Use a spell-check if on a computer, or a good speller if not. Ask someone to read your work to see if it makes sense before handing it in for assessment.
Student cannot quote from the text properly	Either quotations are far too long or so short they show nothing. Quotations are not introduced or no conclusion is drawn about them so they seem to be filling space not adding to the essay.	Make sure any quotation is relevant to a point you wish to make. Do not use too many quotations; the essay is supposed to be mainly your words not the author's.
Student is using vocabulary that is too simple for Year 12 level	Using 'word' where a more appropriate technical term would be better, e.g. verb, noun, adjective, adverb etc. Failing to use appropriate figures of speech e.g. simile, metaphor, imagery, alliteration, at least some of the time.	Know the essential technical terms. They are in the Language Lists at the back of this book.
Student is parroting a learned essay	Sentences do not fit together well, varying from the complex structure of the copied essay to the often simple structure of the student's. Essay does not really fit the question.	Think for yourself and know the text well. ANSWER THE QUESTION! ANSWER THE QUESTION! ANSWER THE QUESTION!

ISBN 9780170244213

Resources

Sometimes you may need a little help and there is help at hand. There are useful books of literary criticism of the works of major authors in your school and public library. Look on the shelves at 809 using the Dewey Decimal System. (By the way, *criticism* means *comment on, analysis of,* not being critical of). Reading what other professionals think of the texts you are studying can help inform your own understanding, provided you have read the text carefully (and more than once) yourself first.

Watching a film adaptation of a novel or reading a chapter summary is never the same experience as reading the novel for yourself!

We know (and we know that you know!) that there is a lot of material on the Internet, too. A summary of chapters can help you get to grips with a long complex novel, reading other students' work on a text might help you sort out your own ideas. But **never** copy work from the Internet. If you use the words of a literary critic they must be acknowledged by using inverted commas around the words and referencing who wrote them.

Just remember that anyone can write on the net and anyone often does. Be sure that what you are reading is the work of someone who knows about the text. Test what they say against what you have observed yourself. In the end, it's *your* understanding that counts, so **write your own essay** from your own knowledge, observations, thoughts and opinions.

An aside on ... the words 'convincingly' and 'perceptively'

There are always words to describe the assessment of your work. Sometimes, at first glance, these might not make much sense to you. Take the word 'convincingly'. If you are going to 'convincingly analyse' the significant connections across texts what does this mean? Basically it means to make points that the marker can see some clear basis to. The marker needs to be that what you say can be supported by the text.

'Perceptively' is another one of these words. Here you will be expected to offer reasoned points that develop understandings that show some insight or originality in thought or interpretation.

As we keep saying, what you think counts. So you have to think!

Writing about written text

Preparation

Let's assume that you have read the text, (more than once would be good, and yes, even a novel can be read more than once!). You have discussed it in class, you have made some notes perhaps or annotated the text if it is short like a poem or a lyric.

ISBN 9780170244213

Step 1

Understand the question

- A question may specify the **main character** or allow you to select **a character** from the text.
- A question may ask about a **conflict** or a **challenge** or a **choice** made by a character. Therefore the text you choose must have a conflict, challenge or choice for you to write about.
- A question may ask you simply to 'show how an **idea** has been developed'. The simplest seeming topics are often the hardest to control and the ones most likely to trap you into merely telling the story. This is the 'theme' question. Choose a theme that is clear to you. You should be able to:
  - clearly explain it in a sentence or two
  - be able to expand on this description
  - give detail on several key places where this theme is revealed.
- Many questions ask you to talk about a specific element (character, setting, style) in connection with the themes/purposes/ideas of a text. If there are **multiple themes** being presented by the author make sure you have a detailed understanding of at least two or three of them. In the external assessment you may find that one theme works better with a certain question over another.
- A question may invite you to write about **more than one text**. If you tackle a question like this then be sure that both texts can be used to answer the question relatively equally.
- A question may ask directly for the **way a text has influenced you personally**. This is still a literature essay, not an invitation to bare your soul! Be sure to keep the text at the forefront of the essay while referring to how it has made you think about an idea.

Step 2

Highlight key instructions in the question

A question may have more than one part and each part needs to be addressed in your answer.

Step 3

Brainstorm

A graphic with a few words could help you quickly sort out if you have enough information to answer the question.

There is a saying 'Don't teach your grandmother to suck eggs' which means don't tell people how to do what they already know how to do. But if you think you need a bit more help at this stage then go back to **Achievement English @ Year 11** and see pages 95–112 for more advice.

Step 4

Plan

When you have **planned your essay** (that is, BEFORE you begin to write it) check that you have covered all aspects of the question. If you haven't, then you may have **chosen the wrong question** to answer. In that case, start over.

Step 5

Edit, spell check, get a reader's opinion

Students often find it very difficult to do this but if you can take constructive criticism it helps a lot. Of course, in an exam you have to be your own critic. Always read through your work before moving on to the next task. If there is time at the end of an assessment, always use it to check your work again.

ISBN 9780170244213

Writing about Visual Text

All of these points apply to writing about text in general but writing about visual text has some additional complexities. When you read a novel, short story or poem, the writer describes things for you, but your imagination changes these into images; things like scenery, clothes, characters' appearances, facial expressions etc. In a visual text you are watching someone else's creation of these images, and there is a whole set of technical terms to explain this creation. Many you will already know. Some may be new to you.

Film techniques

You know that film has a whole technical vocabulary of its own. You will notice that again we have a circle in the left hand margin. Read through the list and tick any techniques that you can refer to when discussing the film you have studied in class.

○ **BIRD'S EYE VIEW**
A shot in which the camera photographs a scene from directly overhead.

○ **CLOSE-UP**
A detailed view of a person or object, usually without much context provided.

○ **CONTINUITY**
The smooth transitions between shots, when space and time are unobtrusively condensed.

○ **CRANE SHOT**
A shot taken from a special device called a crane, which resembles a huge mechanical arm. The crane carries the camera and operator, and can move in virtually any direction.

○ **CROSS CUTTING**
The alternating of shots from two sequences, often in different locations, to suggest the sequences are taking place simultaneously.

○ **DEEP FOCUS**
A technique of photography which permits all distance planes to remain clearly in focus, from close-up range to infinity.

○ **DISSOLVE**
The slow fading out of one shot and the gradual fading in of its successor, with a superimposition of images, usually at the midpoint.

○ **DOLLY SHOT/TRACKING SHOT/TRUCKING**
A shot taken from a moving vehicle. Originally tracks were laid on the set to permit a smoother movement of the camera. A smooth hand-held travelling shot is considered a variation of the dolly shot.

○ **EDITING**
The joining of one shot (strip of film) with another. The shots can picture events and objects in different places at different times.

○ **ESTABLISHING SHOT**
Usually an extreme long or long shot offered at the beginning of a scene or sequence providing the viewer with a context for subsequent closer shots.

○ **EXTREME CLOSE-UP**
A minutely detailed view of an object or a person. An extreme close-up of an actor generally includes only the eyes, or mouth.

○ **EXTREME LONG SHOT**
A panoramic view of an exterior location, photographed from a great distance.

○ **EYE LEVEL SHOT**
The placement of the camera at approximately the corresponding height of an observer on the scene.

○ **FISH EYE LENS**
An extreme wide angle lens, which distorts the image so radically that the edges seem wrapped into a sphere.

○ **FLASH EDITING**
Editing sequences so that the duration of the shots are very brief.

○ **FULL SHOT**
A type of long shot which includes the human body in full, with the head near the top of the frame and the feet near the bottom.

○ **HIGH ANGLE SHOT**
A shot in which the subject is photographed from above.

○ **LONG SHOT**
Includes an amount of picture within the frame which roughly corresponds to the audience's view of the area within the proscenium arch of the traditional theatre.

○ **LONG TAKE**
A shot of lengthy duration.

ISBN 9780170244213

○ **LOW ANGLE SHOT**
A shot in which the subject is photographed from below.

○ **MASTER SHOT**
A single uninterrupted shot, usually taken from a long or full shot range, which contains an entire scene. Later, the closer shots are photographed, and an edited sequence, composed of a variety of different shots, is subsequently constructed on the editor's bench.

○ **MEDIUM SHOT**
A relatively close shot, revealing a moderate amount of detail. A medium shot of a figure generally includes the body from the knees or waist up.

○ **MISE-EN-SCÈNE**
The arrangement of volumes and movements within a given space. In the cinema, the space is defined by the frame; in the traditional theatre, usually by the proscenium arch.

○ **MONTAGE**
A transitional sequence of rapidly edited images, used to suggest the lapse of time or the passing of events. Often employs dissolves and multiple exposures.

○ **OBLIQUE ANGLE**
A shot which is photographed by a tilted camera. When the image is projected on the screen, the subject itself seems to be tilted on its side.

○ **OVER-THE-SHOULDER SHOT**
A medium shot, useful in dialogue scenes, in which one actor is photographed face-on from over the shoulder of another actor.

○ **POINT-OF-VIEW SHOT**
Any shot which is taken from the vantage point of a character in the film. Also known as the first person camera.

○ **PULL BACK DOLLY**
A technique used to surprise the viewer by withdrawing from a scene to reveal an object or character that was previously out of the frame.

○ **REACTION SHOT**
A cut to a shot of a character's reaction to the contents of the preceding shot.

○ **REVERSE ANGLE SHOT**
A shot taken from an angle 180° opposed to the previous shot. That is, the camera is reversed and placed opposite its previous position.

○ **SCENE**
A unit of film composed of a number of interrelated shots, unified usually by a central concern such as a location, an incident, or a minor dramatic climax.

○ **SELECTIVE FOCUSING**
The blurring of focal planes in sequence, forcing the viewer's eye to 'travel' with those areas of an image that remain in sharp focus.

○ **SHOT**
Those images which are recorded continuously from the time the camera starts to the time it stops. That is, an unedited, uncut strip of film.

○ **SUB-TEXT**
A term used in drama and film to signify the dramatic implications beneath the language of a play or movie. Often the sub text concerns ideas and emotions that are totally independent of the language of a text.

○ **TELEPHOTO LENS, LONG LENS**
A lens which acts as a telescope, magnifying the size of objects at a great distance.

○ **THREE-SHOT**
A medium shot, featuring three actors.

○ **TWO-SHOT**
A medium shot, featuring two actors.

○ **WIDE ANGLE LENS**
A lens which permits the camera to photograph a wider area than a normal lens. A significant side effect is its tendency to exaggerate perspective. Also used for deep-focus photography.

○ **WIPE**
An editing device, usually a line which travels across the screen, 'pushing off' one image and revealing another.

○ **ZOOM LENS**
A lens of variable focal length which permits the camera operator to change from wide angle to telephoto shots (and vice versa) in one continuous movement.

○ **ZOOM SHOT**
A shot taken with the aid of a zoom lens. The lens changes focal length during the shot so that a dolly or crane shot can be used.

ISBN 9780170244213

HOWEVER ... a visual text is still a text!

Points to remember

- Use the **correct terminology** for the medium. A character in a film wears a costume, for example. A section of film is a scene, in a novel it is a chapter.
- You are still writing about a **text** and accurately quoting from the text and making relevant references to it are just as important as when you are writing about a novel or a short story.

Step 1

Understand the question

- Questions are not so different from those for written texts (see above) but they will require you to consider the **pictures** as well as the **words** and sometimes the question makes this clear, as in this sample question: *How are **verbal and visual** features of a text (or texts) used to give audiences a strong idea?*
- Even if this distinction is not specified in the question, you still need to refer to **words and pictures** if you are writing about a visual text.
- Of course, oral features like **tone of voice** come into oral text analysis too.

Step 2

Highlight key instructions in the question

A question may have more than one part and each part needs to be addressed in your answer.

Step 3

Brainstorm

A simple graphic with a few words could help you quickly sort out if you have enough information to answer the question.

Step 4

Plan

When you have **planned your essay** (that is, BEFORE you begin to write it) check that you have covered all aspects of the question. If you haven't, then you may have **chosen the wrong question** to answer. In that case, start over.

Part of getting better is practice but it is also getting critical feedback and applying it to the next effort. Even if you are struggling, always hand an essay in when the teacher asks. For a start they are more likely to take more time helping you than someone who never hands anything in. Alongside this you will get valuable comments written on your essay and be able to apply any general class comments directly to your own work.

Step 5

Edit, spell check, get a reader's opinion

Students often find it very difficult to do this but if you can take constructive criticism it helps a lot. Of course, in an exam you have to be your own critic. Always read through your work before moving on to the next task. And if there is time at the end of an assessment, use it to check your work again.

ISBN 9780170244213

12 Language Lists

Although we have divided these techniques into lists linking them to specific text type, they may well be relevant to more than one type of text. For example, you might find a rhetorical question in a speech, a formal essay, a poem or a magazine article.

Language techniques for written text

ABSTRACT NOUN

Name of something that we cannot see, touch or measure. You can give it … but you can't wrap it up.

E.g. air, authority, amazement

ADJECTIVE

An adjective describes a noun. Adds detail to names and nouns.

E.g. black, bold, big, brave, bronzed

ADVERB

Gives you more information about a verb. Adverbs tell you when, where or how something is done.

E.g. cheerfully, thirstily, happily, miserably

ALLUSION

An indirect reference to a person or event. These may be, but are not necessarily, people and events in mythology and history. An allusion can create an added dimension to an image often by a comparison between similar qualities in the subject and in what is being alluded to.

E.g. 'Sticky wicket' is a difficult situation demanding coolness and judgement. An allusion to the game of cricket.

CLICHÉ

Trite and worn out phrases that communicate an image easily, and don't need too much thinking about.

E.g. I could eat a horse.

COLLECTIVE NOUN

Name of a group of objects, people or creatures. A collection of similar things or people – that is why it's called a collective noun.

E.g. band, orchestra, ensemble, quartet, group

COLLOQUIAL LANGUAGE

The word colloquial is used to define language that is used in casual conversation. It is likely to be even more ungrammatical, fractured and full of cliché than informal language. You will use colloquial expressions in your everyday conversations with friends and family.

E.g. G'day. You coming out? I'm off now.

COMMON NOUN

Name of ordinary, everyday objects. Can be preceded by 'a/an' or 'the'.

E.g. a pear, an apple, the banana

COMPARATIVE ADJECTIVE

A form of adjective that compares things. Shows the difference between two things.

E.g. blacker, bolder, bigger, braver, more bronzed

CONJUNCTION

A conjunction links two or more sentences into a single sentence. Known as a 'joining word'. Conjunctions are usually found in the middle of sentences, but not always. Conjunctions can also join words, phrases or clauses.

E.g. and, so, but, yet, or, after, because

CONNOTATION

Connotation is the implied or suggested meaning of the word. It is the opposite of denotation, which is the dictionary definition.

DENOTATION

The dictionary definition of the word. It is the opposite of *connotation* which is the implied or suggested meaning.

EMOTIVE LANGUAGE

Words designed to evoke an emotional response in the reader.

EUPHEMISM

A euphemism expresses an unpleasant or uncomfortable or embarrassing situation in a more sensitive, kind and tactful manner. The purpose is to soften the blow, protect feelings or to be politically correct.

E.g. My grandfather passed away.

HYPERBOLE

Deliberate exaggeration.

IRONY

The method of expression in which the ordinary meaning of the word is more or less the opposite of what the speaker/writer intends. For example: In *Pride and Prejudice* by Jane Austen, Mr Bennett stops his daughter Mary from playing any longer on the piano at a party by saying 'That will do extremely well, child. You have delighted us long enough.' It might seem like praise on the surface but is not; Mary plays poorly and is disconcerted by her father's words. The effect of irony draws attention to the real meaning behind the words and may convey a character or writer's attitude. Irony may also be used to create humour.

JARGON

Jargon is used by a particular group, profession or culture. Often, other people do not understand the words and so it can seem like pretentious or meaningless language.

Jargon may be highly technical.

E.g. My new bike is awesome. It has a Cro-mo frame and alloy rims and the groupset are all high spec'd. I got semi-slicks but they threw in some knobblies, too.

ISBN 9780170244213

NARRATIVE VOICE
Narrative means telling of events.
Novels and short stories may be written in the third person (he walked along the road ... she ate a red apple ... they went to the movies together). The writer may present information about these characters by describing what they do or where they are. They may mix dialogue in with narrative to show what the characters think or feel. The writer may choose to show what just one character thinks and feels and leave the reader to make their own minds up about the other characters. The writer may choose to reveal everything about everyone. This is called the omniscient narrator or eye-of-god technique.

NOUN
Naming word.
E.g. plum, Peter, power, pod

PREPOSITION
A preposition tells us the position or place of something in relation to something else. Prepositions are usually 'small words'.
E.g. at, by, for, on, in, of, under

PROPER NOUN
Name of person, place etc. Always begins with a capital letter.
E.g. Alan to Zebedee, Africa to Zanzibar

PRONOUN
A pronoun is used in the place of a noun. Avoids always repeating a name.
E.g. I, me, mine, you, yours

PUN
A pun is a clever play on words which are similar in sound but different meaning. The double meaning is used to convey humour. Puns are often used in headlines, advertising, jokes and riddles.
E.g. P&O holidays: living the cruisy lifestyle

SLANG
Slang is very informal language that is usually vivid, playful and short-lived. Each generation formulates its own slang and these words are usually 'passing phases'. We would have given you an example but it would be out-of-date before the book was printed!

SUPERLATIVE ADJECTIVE
A form of adjective that describes the best or the most from three or more things. It's also pointing out difference.
E.g. blackest, boldest, biggest, bravest, most bronzed

SYNTAX
Syntax is a word derived from Greek, which means 'to put in order'. It is a branch of grammar dealing with:
a the arrangement of words in sentences
b the correct use of parts of speech
c the classification of sentences according to their clause structure.

TENSE
The form of the verb that indicates the time of the action. There are three main tenses; past, present and future.

VERB
A word that expresses doing or being. Somebody or something does something. Something or somebody is something.
E.g. I eat, I drink, I am (happy), I was (thirsty)

See also: Language techniques for poetic text

Language techniques for poetic text

ALLITERATION
Alliteration is the repetition of consonant sounds at the beginning of words placed closely together to create a sound echo.
E.g. A black-backed gull bent like an iron bar slowly
This line has to be read slowly in order to pronounce the words. Therefore it emphasises the strength of the wind against which the bird is flying.
Alliteration is used to:
- add humour or power
- create a mood or feeling
- help the flow or movement of language. Some alliteration is hard ... b and d, while others are soft, calming ... l, s, f
- emphasise important points

ANTITHESIS
Placing contrasting terms or ideas close together to emphasise their difference and give the effect of balance.
E.g. To err is human, to forgive, divine.
For fools rush in where angels fear to tread.
(Alexander Pope)

APOSTROPHE
A direct address to a person or personified idea.
E.g. Death, be not proud (John Donne)
Oh grave! Where is thy victory?
Oh death! Where is thy sting? (Book of Isaiah, The Bible)
Use of apostrophe creates the effect of a cry, an outpouring of emotion.

ASSONANCE
Assonance is the repetition of vowel sounds. The trick is not to think of it as the same letter, but the same sound.
E.g.
He climbed high, singing wildly
Clinging to the rock face
Alive, at last.
As with alliteration, assonance allows the poem to flow more quickly or it can slow the poem down as each word is emphasised to reflect the meaning of that part of the poem. Note: assonance is not rhyme! In fact true assonance is where the consonants following the vowels are different.

CAESURA
A natural pause or a break in a line of poetry, usually indicated by a punctuation mark.
E.g. When will the bell ring, and end this weariness?
(D.H. Lawrence, Last Lesson of the Afternoon)

END-STOPPED LINE
The lines of a stanza that have a grammatical pause at the end of a line.
E.g. I can haul and urge them no more.
(D.H. Lawrence, Last Lesson of the Afternoon)
This technique completes an idea visually and grammatically.

ENJAMBMENT
When the meaning of a line of poetry is completed on the next line.
E.g. How long have they tugged the leash, and strained apart,
My pack of unruly hounds. (D.H. Lawrence, Last Lesson of the Afternoon)
This technique can emphasise an idea or add to the rhythm and flow of the lines.

ISBN 9780170244213

EXTENDED METAPHOR
This is a metaphor that is extended over a passage or throughout a poem.

IMAGERY
The creation of images or pictures to help writers achieve their intended purpose. An image can be created using different devices such as similes, assonance or adjectives.

METAPHOR
A metaphor is a comparison which does not use 'like' or 'as'. It says that one thing is another.
E.g. My brother John is a pig.
This metaphor suggests that John has unpleasant manners, not that he actually is a pig. Metaphors are used to highlight certain qualities of whatever is being described.

ONOMATOPOEIA
Onomatopoeia uses words that imitate and reproduce real-life sounds and actions.
E.g. The buzz of a chainsaw.
Onomatopoeia helps to increase reality in the text through adding another dimension by suggesting sound as well as meaning. Onomatopoeic words are often found in comic strips.

OXYMORON
Two words or phrases of opposite or contrasting meaning placed together for effect.
E.g. Parting is such sweet sorrow. (William Shakespeare, Romeo and Juliet)
This suggests that the two lovers are sad to be parting but this sadness is to be enjoyed a little as they anticipate being together again.

PERSONIFICATION
Personification is where a non-living object is given living qualities, writing of it as if it were a living person. Appearances, actions, thoughts and feelings can all be given human attributes. Personification gives life and energy to images and ideas.
E.g. The vine is strangling that tree.
This gives the idea of the vine as an aggressor with intent to harm and the tree as the victim.

REPETITION
When words or phrases are repeated for emphasis of some kind.
E.g. Veni, vidi, vici. I came, I saw, I conquered. (Julius Caesar)
Repetition is often used for emphasis and in this case Caesar is pointing out his own importance.

RHYME
Rhyme is the repetition of final vowel and consonant sounds in words.
E.g.
She left the web, she left the loom,
She made three paces thro' the room,
She saw the water-lily bloom,
(from The Lady of Shallot, Alfred Lord Tennyson)
In this poem the rhyming words at the end of each line match well the rhythm and harshness of the poem's meaning. Words that sound the same, or almost the same, are likely to make us notice them. Rhyming words can fall anywhere, in the middle of lines, in regular or irregular patterns, but we are most used to them at the end of lines of poetry.

Rhyme is designed to:

- add pleasing sound effects
- provide a disciplined structure
- highlight particular words/phrases
- follow an established pattern.

RHYTHM
The rhythm is the flow and beat of the poem.
E.g.
This is the night mail crossing the border
Bringing the cheque and the postal order
(from The Night Mail, W.H Auden)
Here the beat/sound of the train is imitated.

SIBILANCE
The repetition of the consonant s or z to give a hissing sound. The effect of sibilance is to slow the reader as s and z take longer to say. This, in turn, emphasises the idea and can also create an onomatopoeic effect.
E.g. suggesting snake like movement and sound – 'slippery, slithering, sliding snake'.

SIMILE
A simile is a direct comparison that always contains the word 'as' or 'like'.
E.g. My brother John eats like a pig.
This suggests that John has unpleasant table manners. A simile adds vivid, descriptive details.

SYMBOLISM
A word or phrase signifying a sign or mark representing something else.
E.g. The dove (of peace), the cross (of Christianity)
A symbol conveys a significant idea and all its connotations through use of a single word.

Language techniques for visual text

ACRONYM
A pronounceable word created by taking the initial letters of a series of words.
E.g. SADD = Students Against Drunk Driving
ANZAC = Australia New Zealand Army Corps

ALLITERATION
Alliteration is easy to remember. The audience will be able to recall the catch phrase at another time. Alliteration also makes words flow together more easily and it can highlight key words and ideas.
E.g. Just Juice, NZ Natural

BACKGROUND
The background may be left plain in order to focus the viewer's attention onto the other features or it may incorporate colour to support its message.
E.g. A green background on an advertisement for a healthy product is not uncommon, for example, as green suggests natural. Faint images which link to the message of the whole poster or advertisement may be used as background.

BALANCE
Designers achieve balance by looking at a layout design as an arrangement of shapes. The easiest way to create balance in a visual text is to treat all the elements as geometric shapes.

ISBN 9780170244213

BODY COPY
Body copy is usually found in a paragraph towards the bottom of an image. These detailed words in a static image are often referred to as the 'small print'.

BOLD LINES
Bold shapes and lines help to draw in the eye. Some things are outlined in black to give them definition or to frame certain parts of the whole image.

CARICATURE
Characterisation that exaggerates certain features for comic effect.

COLOUR
Colours help represent a product or an idea.
E.g. An advertisement for berry yoghurt is likely to be based around pinks and purples to help represent the product. An image designed to sell a cleaning product is likely to have a lot of white to suggest cleanliness.

CONTRAST
Use of two colours for eye-catching contrasts. Designers think about which colours combine effectively. For instance yellow & black, red & black, orange & purple.
E.g. Football team uniforms.

DVF
The Dominant Visual Feature is the central focus of the static image. The point of impact. It may be dominant because of its position, often at the centre of the image.

EMPTY SPACE
Empty space refers to areas of the text that have no text or graphics in them. These areas may not necessarily be printed in the colour 'white', but it is important the colour is the same throughout so that the effect works in the same way.
Empty space is used to:
- prevent the layout looking crowded
- help balance the overall design
- create impact or focus on a certain feature
- help the audience to read the text and graphics in the correct order.

FONT (STYLE AND SIZE)
Designers choose the fonts of the text to go with their images carefully. The text must be clear to read (not too elaborate) and in some situations, able to be read from a distance. The font will also aim to reflect the ideas within the image.
E.g. In advertising a children's product the font will be large and colourful while a funeral home is likely to choose an elegant, simple font.

GRAPHIC/ILLUSTRATION
Graphics are the pictures, photographs, drawings, graphs - everything that is not the writing in an image.

HEADLINE
The headline is the main 'title' of the advertisement/image. This will be in the biggest font size. Subheadings, in smaller print, may be used, too. The words are designed to attract attention and provoke the audience to look further.

HIERARCHY
The hierarchy of a layout design means the order of importance of different elements and the order in which elements should be viewed or read. When each element is given a grade of importance and designers style or size them as such, it makes it easy for readers to know where to look or read first and where to move their eyes across and into the visual.

LAYOUT
Layout is the process of organising forms, shapes, colours and any words into a balanced design. These choices are made with the purpose, topic and audience in mind.

LEVEL OF LANGUAGE (FORMAL, INFORMAL, COLLOQUIAL, SLANG, JARGON)
The type of language chosen for an advertisement gives us clues about the intended audience.
- If it is simple it could be aimed at children.
- If it is feminine and flowery it is most likely aimed at girls or women.
- If it is chatty and conversational it is most likely advertising something we would use everyday.
- If it is formal it is most likely advertising something of a serious nature.
- If there is a lot of technical language it would have a very specific audience in mind, for example modern computer users or car fanatics.
- A lot of slang terms might indicate it is aimed at a youthful audience.

PERSONAL PRONOUNS
Personal pronouns are used to make the audience feel that the advertisement is speaking directly to them. They give a chatty, conversational tone to the piece to make the audience feel included.

PUN
A pun is a clever play on words, using two words that are alike in sound but different in meaning. The double meaning is used to convey humour. Headlines make use of puns in order to grab attention.
E.g. Trust British Paints ... Sure Can.
New Indian Restaurant Curries Favour

REPETITION
Repetition aids memory, whether it is to donate money to World Vision or to buy Five Brothers pasta sauce. Repeating the product name, slogan and/or key features will help people remember the brand.

RHETORICAL QUESTION
A rhetorical question expects no answer because it assumes one. It is used to allow the audience to focus on and consider the posed question.
E.g. Sick of spending hours scrubbing your shower and it still not being clean?
The assumed answer to this question is 'Of course, I am.'

RULE OF THIRDS
The rule states that an image can be divided into nine equal parts by two equally-spaced horizontal lines and two equally spaced vertical lines. The four points formed by the intersections of these lines can be used to align features in a visual image.

Designers believe the Rule of Thirds creates more tension, energy and interest in the image than simply centering the feature would. Following the rule also helps produce balanced picture/images.

SLOGAN
Most companies and services have a slogan (a short, snappy sentence) that is easy to remember. You probably know where it is claimed that 'everyone gets a bargain'.

ISBN 9780170244213

SYMBOLS/LOGOS

Symbolism is where a concrete object is used to represent one or more abstract ideas. It can be words, a shape, a graphic. *E.g. The dove (a material object) represents peace (something abstract). White crosses may represent road accident victims.* Most companies and services have a logo (graphic drawing/symbol) that represents their company, from the Nike whoosh to the MacDonald's M.

In the same way that 'a picture is worth a thousand words' so a symbol or a logo can bring to mind a whole range of thoughts and feelings.

UNUSUAL IMAGES

Unusual pictures or layout to make people stop and study the image more closely may be used.

THE VERBAL/VISUAL LINK

Whenever a visual text is put together there is always a strong focus on the links that exist between the verbal and the visual elements.

USE OF ADJECTIVES

Advertisers will often choose words that help us picture the look, taste or texture of the product. Think about what advertisers say about breakfast cereals: *crunchy, wholesome, nutty, tasty*.

Comparative adjectives like *'better'* and *'kinder'* and *'creamier'* are often used.

Superlatives are common, too. Think about the words *'crumbliest, flakiest'* which are superlative adjectives. You are probably thinking Cadbury's chocolate!

WELL-KNOWN/POPULAR FACES

Many advertisements use someone who is famous to sell a product/service. It may be purely to attract attention *(for example Dan Carter selling underwear)* or it may be endorsing a product that the celebrity would know about *(for example David Beckham advertising soccer boots).*

Language techniques for oral text

ALLUSION/REFERENCE

An indirect reference to an event or person.

E.g. Five score years ago ...' alludes to the opening of Lincoln's Gettysburg address and its statement of equality and freedom.

The effect is to extend an image or idea in the listener's mind.

ANAPHORA

Repetition of a word or phrase in successive clauses.

E.g. 'I have a dream.'

'Let freedom ring...' (Martin Luther King)

The effect is often one of emphasis.

ANECDOTES

Telling a short story (based on either fact or fiction) can help to illustrate a point. Speakers often use these to keep their audience interested and listening because we all enjoy stories. *E.g. 'A young girl had to be removed from her school because of all the merciless text bullying she was receiving She would break down in tears during class time, and she threatened to commit suicide on several occasions ...'*

ANTITHESIS

The contrast between words or ideas. Used to emphasise a difference and/or to give the effect of balance.

E.g. He knew everything about literature except how to enjoy it.' (Catch 22 by Joseph Heller)

'I come to bury Caesar, not to praise him.
The evil that men do lives after them;
The good is oft interred with their bones;'
(Mark Antony in Shakespeare's Julius Caesar)

'The love of liberty is the love of others; the love of power is the love of ourselves.' (William Hazlitt, 19th century journalist)

AUDIENCE APPEAL

A good speaker knows their audience before they begins and reads their audience as they speak. A student wanting to be voted onto their school's Board of Trustees will talk about current issues facing students at that school. An aspiring politican wanting to be voted in by a community facing a major issue (e.g., West Coast: logging, Waihi: mining) will talk about that issue above all else.

EMOTIVE WORDS

These are words which have strong feelings, or emotions, associated with them. These emotions can be positive or negative. Such words set the tone of voice which expresses the speaker's attitude to a person or topic. E.g. 'sunny, hopeful and healthy' versus 'grim, disgusting, and dangerous'.

Positive words create a sense of confidence and optimism about an argument. Negative words can suggest disapproval or pessimism.

E.g. 'A young girl had to be removed from her school because of all the merciless text bullying she was receiving.'

INFORMAL LANGUAGE

Chatty, colloquial phrases help relax the audience and make them feel involved. Speech-writers will often use clichés, contractions, colloquial phrases in order to do this.

E.g. 'How weird is that?' ...

LISTING

Listing is where speakers will 'list' several examples at once. Providing an audience with a lot of examples adds weight to your argument. It is also an economical way of getting a lot of information across quickly.

E.g. 'My cellphone; my small, stylish, splendid, spectacularly useful cellphone.'

PARALLELISM

Comparison or correspondence of two successive passages:

'On the 4th of July we count our blessings, and there are so many to count. We're thankful for the families we love. We're thankful for the opportunities in America. We're thankful for our freedom ...' (George W. Bush, 4 July 2002)

Did you know that the mathematical sign for equals was invented by someone who said that nothing is more similar or equal than two parallel lines?

PERSONAL PRONOUNS

A speaker uses personal pronouns to involve his or her audience. By using 'you' the speech comes across as being aimed directly at the audience, as though the speaker is talking to individual members of the audience.

'We' and 'our' are also commonly used by a speech-writer to encourage the audience to think the speaker is one of them and therefore makes them feel included. This in turn makes the speech seem more personal.

ISBN 9780170244213

E.g: 'As teenagers we hold one thing above all others. On thing we cannot live without. One thing we spend most of our hard-earned cash on.

QUOTATIONS

Quoting well-known people may give a speech a greater air of authority.

Quotations work well at the beginning or end of a speech as they can make people pay more attention to the idea being expressed.

E.g. '"We're very concerned about reports of TXT bullying and are committed to helping young people fight this," says Vodafone general manager of communications and sponsorship, Lynley Kirk-Smith:'

REFERENCES TO AUTHORITY

Referring to people, groups or companies that have authority helps make the audience believe your claims as they know the source is reputable. Groups such as the Police, United Nations, Governments, Greenpeace, Amnesty International fall into this category.

E.g. 'Organisations like NetSafe want to make sure that young people don't feel helpless and ensure that they're aware of the practical steps they can take to help themselves ...'

REPETITION

Speech writers (just like poets and visual designers) employ the repetition of words or phrases in order to emphasise a main point. It may be a point repeated several times throughout the speech to ensure that it is emphasised or it may be the first word or phrase repeated for emphasis.

E.g. Gone are the days when students ***avoided certain*** *areas of the mall,* ***certain*** *toilet blocks in the school,* ***avoided certain*** *routes home.*

RHETORICAL QUESTION

A rhetorical question is a question where the answer is implied. It adds to the persuasive power of the speaker. Often a speaker adds emphasis to a point by putting it in the form of a question, the answer to which supports his or her argument.

Rhetorical questions are designed to get the audience to momentarily stop and think about what is being said. This in turn involves them in the speech and encourages them to keep listening so they can hear what the answer will be. It is essential for there to be a pause after a rhetorical question to allow this thought to take place.

E.g. What is this one indispensable thing? Need I tell you? It is this – the cellphone.

A rhetorical question may also be used effectively at the beginning or end of a speech. It either engages the audience immediately or leaves them with something to think about. This may provoke them to make a change in their lives or to consider the issue beyond the end of a speech.

TRICOLON

The division of an idea into three harmonious parts, usually of increasing power.

E.g. '... government of the people, by the people, for the people' (Abraham Lincoln, President of the USA, in the Gettysburg Address at the dedication of a graveyard at Gettysburg, one of the battlefields of the American Civil War in 1863.)

'Today, our fellow citizens, our way of life, our very freedom came under attack ...' (George Bush, President of the USA, in his address to the nation after the terrorist attack on New York, 11 September 2001.)

USE OF HUMOUR

One of the most powerful tools a speech-writer has is humour. We all like to laugh. It must be appropriate to the subject matter though.

E.g. 'My cellphone; my small, stylish, splendid, spectacularly useful cellphone.'

USE OF STATISTICS

Using statistics helps to support ideas with fact. They can convince the audience that there is verifiable support for an argument.

E.g. 'Last year, Vodafone alone received 4600 complaints about text bullying.'

See also: Language techniques for poetic text

ISBN 9780170244213

Use this space to list any additional language techniques introduced to you by your teacher.

ISBN 9780170244213

13

Revision

It's time to revise – ready, set, go!

External assessment for English is likely to be one of the first assessments you sit. A lot of students sit this assessment and the markers need time to get all the papers marked!

You will be offered the following external standards:

AS 2.1 Show understanding of specified aspect(s) of studied written text(s), using supporting evidence

AS 2.2 Show understanding of specified aspect(s) of studied visual or oral text(s), using supporting evidence

AS 2.3 Show understanding of significant aspects of unfamiliar written text(s) through close reading, using supporting evidence

We have assumed that you will be preparing for each Standard. We have met students who say: "*Well, I'll just prepare for the two I think I can do best in.*" This is NOT a good idea. Seriously. What if that particular Standard asks questions that really don't work for your text/s? What if you don't really understand a question? What if you panic and go blank about a text? Our best advice is to **prepare for all the Standards** offered.

Know thyself

You have already experienced revising for external assessment, so you will know what **your personal strengths and weaknesses** are:

Aim to build on your strengths:

- I study best in the mornings.
- I need to eat first then study.
- It's best if I go to the library; so I go.

Aim to minimise your weaknesses:

- I have to turn my phone off.
- I have to promise myself chocolate AFTER I study.
- I have to get Mum to take my sisters to the park for an hour.

Yes, it's true that every student approaches revision in their own way, but there are some things that we think are just as important in Year 12 as they were in Year 11.

ISBN 9780170244213

A place to study

It is important that you set yourself up a study station. You will need a desk or a table, a comfortable (not too comfortable) chair, good lighting ... and quiet. Make sure you have a good stock of refill, pens, pencils and highlighters, too.

If you are not able to work in your bedroom, then using a corner of the dining room table is fine. Turn off the TV. Turn off the radio. Ask Dad to take care of your little brother. You need time and space to think!

A time to study

You probably have lots of things in your life other than school. This is the time of year when you evaluate which of these things are unavoidable and which commitments could be put on hold (or at least reduced) during the lead up to the examinations. Can you work fewer hours? Do you need to attend every team training session? Can you avoid a trip to Aunt Karen's this week?

Set up a personal weekly planner. This is likely to change each week, so create one week at a time and fill in the study you plan to do each week. Your study time may vary depending on what hours you work, your sports or family commitments. Plus, if you are having extra tutoring you can count this towards that subject for the week. You need to ensure though that if you take extra time off, you make it up somewhere else.

We are quite aware that you will have more than just English to study for. You need to work out how many subjects you have to study and the actual commitment each subject will take. The examples we have used assume you have five subjects that will have up to three external assessments each.

We have started this timetable at 9 am but if you are a 'morning person' you might prefer to do an hour's study between 6.30 and 7.30 am!

Timetable 1: For during the school week

	Mon	Tues	Wed	Thurs	Fri	Sat	Sun
9.00-10.00							Biology
10.00-11.00							
11.00-12.00							English
12.00-1.00							
1.00-2.00							Maths
2.00-3.00							
3.00-4.00						English	Geography
4.00-5.00	Geography	Media Studies	Maths	Media Studies		English	
5.00-6.00							Media Studies
6.00-7.00	English	Maths	Biology	Geography			
7.00-8.00							Biology
8.00-9.00							

ISBN 9780170244213

When school finishes you should change your timetable to reflect the increase in the time available for study. Take a look at the example below:

Timetable 2: For when school has finished

	Mon	Tues	Wed	Thurs	Fri	Sat	Sun
9.00-10.00	English	Biology		Media Studies	English		
10.05-11.05		Media Studies	Maths	Geography	Biology		Maths
							English
11.30-12.30	Maths	English	Geography	English	Maths		Media Studies
12.35-1.05	English			Maths			Biology
2.00-3.00	Biology	Maths	Media Studies		Geography	Media Studies	English
3.05-4.00	Media Studies	Geography	Biology	Biology	Media Studies	English	
							Media Studies
4.30-5.30	Geography		English	Biology		Geography	Maths
7.00-8.00							

An aside on ... studying for assessment of your texts

1 Know the text well.
2 Spell its title and author/director's name correctly.
3 Learn a few short quotations that might be used for examples in several essay questions.
4 Know the principal characters' names exactly.
5 List the major theme/themes for revision.
6 Learn details of the setting (time, place, social background).
7 Practise writing to time (you will probably do this in class).

You will notice that there is enough space to add a sixth subject if you need to, or to add extra hours to subjects that you find more difficult. Of course you can vary your timetable to suit your life's pattern.

You need to make sure that when you are not studying that you are doing something other than sitting and watching TV! Getting some fresh air is a great way to recharge your batteries. It could be a swim, a walk (even if only to the letterbox!), a game of basketball etc.

Eat good, healthy food and drink plenty of water. Sleep is also a vital part of a good study programme – burning the midnight oil is not a useful technique for most of us.

What to study

Your classroom teachers will provide you with some ideas for a study programme but we would like to suggest one for English revision that we know is successful.

On pages 170-72 you will find a programme that will incorporate:

- 4 weeks of 4 sessions
- 2 weeks of 7 sessions (or thereabouts!)

By the time you have completed all the sessions you will be prepared for the external examinations.

Your teacher may set activities specific to your class's content, so be flexible and incorporate their requirements into your programme of revision.

How to study

You will also need to have sorted all your material from English classes, revision lessons, personal study, tutoring etc into a divided ring binder or separate folders.

Go through your entire room, bag, books and ask your teacher for any copies of examination essays, or marking that has not been returned to you. If you were absent for any time during the year you need to make sure you have any notes you may have missed. Your friends may be able to help, and your teacher.

You might also decide to spend some time going through the internet and/or library seeing what you can find about your text. There are often websites that give you information about your text. This information can be used to supplement your class notes and offer you some new material to refresh your memory about your text. A word of caution: Examiners are experts at seeing when a student has learnt a response off by heart. They don't appreciate this sort of revision.

Sort all your notes into a logical order. Re-writing scrappy notes tidily is a great way of reminding yourself about the topic.

ISBN 9780170244213

It is also a VERY good idea to re-read any books, novels, short stories, poetry, plays or other written texts you have studied during the year and rewatch the film you will be using. It is amazing how much additional detail you pick up once you know a text well. Plus, by this time at the end of the year, you know what is required to write successful essays and you can find extra information to help you answer questions fully as you re-read or rewatch the text.

You will find blank copies of these grids for you to create your own timetable at www.cengage.co.nz/ach-eng-yr12

An aside on ... studying for assessment of unfamiliar texts

The studies on texts that you have completed through the year will have given you the experience of understanding and responding to texts with guidance. In this assessment you have to use those skills without the benefit of a teacher's voice, your fellow classmates' ideas, or a lot of time. It's a great opportunity to show that you CAN read, understand and analyse text all by yourself. Yes, you can.

1 You will have completed several close reading exercises in class (and through *Achievement English @ Year 12*). Revisiting these texts and the questions you were asked and your answers would be useful.
2 Answer the questions again, improving on your first attempt.
3 Make sure you have the process off by heart:
   - read the text
   - read the questions
   - read the text again
   - annotate the text (on the page in the assessment, in class if allowed)
   - think
   - plan
   - write.

   For some students, this seems like a very long process in an assessment where you just want to get on with answering the question. However, if you follow this process (briskly) you will find that it saves time in the end, because you will know what you want to say when you start to write. It usually means better results, too! Try it out in a class assessment before the real thing.

The sessions

Each session is designed to take you an hour of study. This does not include time to find pencils, sort paperwork, make a cup of cocoa, put out the cat etc. so you need to be organised and ready to begin actual revision.

Note: The revision programme refers to the ***Achievement English @ Year 12 Revision Pack****. You can download this for free from www.cengage.co.nz/ach-eng-y12.*

ISBN 9780170244213

Revision Programme

BEFORE YOU BEGIN	SESSION 1	SESSION 2
You may have studied more than one written text this year. Before you begin you need to decide if you are going to revise all options or only the one you feel most comfortable writing about. If you are revising multiple texts then make sure you evenly divide the sessions between them. You may also find it useful to work back through this book filling in any activities you have not completed. Note: The times allocations given in these sessions are guidelines only. You may need a few extra minutes to finish some of them, but then again we are sure there will be a few that you finish quicker so it will even out in the end!	**Recap your Written Text – Character (40 minutes)** Reread the notes/essays/handouts you have on your written text that are connected to character. You may need to rewrite or reorder this material as you go. **Written Text Essay - Character (20 minutes)** Now you are familiar with your notes write a plan of how you might answer the following question: *Analyse how a main character OR individual matures and takes action in a text (or texts) you have studied.*	**Written Text Essay - Character (1 hour)** Answer the following question using the plan you wrote in Session 1. Don't forget to quickly check over your plan in case you missed something: *Analyse how a main character OR individual matures and takes action in a text (or texts) you have studied.*
SESSION 3	**SESSION 4**	**SESSION 5**
Recap of Close Reading (1 hour) Complete Recap Activity 1 from your downloaded *Achievement English @ Year 12 Revision Pack.* Complete Close Reading Activity 1 from your downloaded *Achievement English @ Year 12 Revision Pack.*	**Recap your Written Text – Theme (40 minutes)** Reread the notes/essays/handouts you have on your written text that are connected to theme. You may need to rewrite or reorder this material as you go. **Written Text Essay – Theme (20 minutes)** Now you are familiar with your notes write a plan of how you might answer one of the following questions: 1. *Analyse how symbols are used to develop an idea in a text (or texts) you have studied.* *OR* 2. *Analyse how an idea is developed in a text (or texts) you have studied.*	**Written Text Essay – Theme (1 hour)** Answer the following question using the plan you wrote in Session 4. Don't forget to quickly check over your plan in case you missed something: 1. *Analyse how symbols are used to develop an idea in a text (or texts) you have studied.* *OR* 2. *Analyse how an idea is developed in a text (or texts) you have studied.*
SESSION 6	**SESSION 7**	**SESSION 8**
Close Reading Recap (1 hour) Complete Recap Activity 2 from your downloaded *Achievement English @ Year 12 Revision Pack.* Complete Close Reading Activity 2 from your downloaded *Achievement English @ Year 12 Revision Pack.*	**Recap your Visual/Oral Text – Theme (40 minutes)** Reread the notes/essays/handouts you have on your visual/oral text that are connected to theme. You may need to rewrite or reorder this material as you go. **Visual/Oral Text Essay – Theme (20 minutes)** Now you are familiar with your notes write a plan of how you might answer one of the following questions: 1. *Analyse how verbal AND visual features of a text (or texts) you have studied are used to give audiences a strong idea.* *OR* 2. *Analyse how successful a text (or texts) you have studied has been in influencing you to think differently about an issue.*	**Visual/Oral Text Essay – Theme (1 hour)** Answer the following question using the plan you wrote in Session 7. Don't forget to quickly check over your plan in case you missed something: 1. *Analyse how verbal AND visual features of a text (or texts) you have studied are used to give audiences a strong idea.* *OR* 2. *Analyse how successful a text (or texts) you have studied has been in influencing you to think differently about an issue.*

ISBN 9780170244213

SESSION 9

Improving your work (1 hour)
Look through your year's work and find an essay (from either class work/previous examinations/study) that you have not done well.

a Reread the essay.

b Reread the comments made by your teacher.

c Using a red pen, mark parts of the essay that you know are not done well.

d Using a different colour pen, mark the parts of the essay you know are done well.

e Spend 10 minutes going through your notes looking for information to improve this essay.

f Rewrite the essay.

SESSION 10

Close Reading Recap (1 hour)
Complete Recap Activity 3 from your downloaded *Achievement English @ Year 12 Revision Pack*.

Complete Close Reading Activity 3 from your downloaded *Achievement English @ Year 12 Revision Pack*.

SESSION 11

Close Reading Recap (1 hour)
Complete Recap Activity 4 from your downloaded *Achievement English @ Year 12 Revision Pack*.

Complete Close Reading Activity 4 from your downloaded *Achievement English @ Year 12 Revision Pack*.

SESSION 12

Spend some time looking back through this book for activities that you have not completed during the year.

If you have completed them all spend time learning the Language Lists on pages 158-163.

TAKE STOCK

You are nearly halfway through your revision. Spend some time re-organising your notes/essays etc. Sort out any essays you want to take in to your teacher to mark and make suggestions for improvement.

Assess the timetable you have set and evaluate if it is working. You may need to make some adjustments to your life if you are struggling to find time to settle down and study. Make adjustments if necessary!

SESSION 13

Close Reading Recap (1 hour)
Complete Recap Activity 5 from your downloaded *Achievement English @ Year 12 Revision Pack*.

Complete Close Reading Activity 5 from your downloaded *Achievement English @ Year 12 Revision Pack*.

SESSION 14

Quick Fire – Written text (1 hour)
Answer one of the following questions as though you are in an examination. You have 1 hour to complete the essay – don't forget to plan!

1. *Analyse how the growth OR breakdown of a relationship(s) affects the climax in a text (or texts) you have studied.*

   OR

2. *Analyse how the setting of a text (or texts) you have studied influenced your understanding of the ideas in the text (or texts). (Note: Setting may include reference to time, place, historical or social context, or atmosphere.)*

SESSION 15

Close Reading Recap (1 hour)
Complete Recap Activity 6 from your downloaded *Achievement English @ Year 12 Revision Pack*.

Complete Close Reading Activity 6 from your downloaded *Achievement English @ Year 12 Revision Pack*.

SESSION 16

Recap your Visual/Oral Text – Character (40 minutes)
Reread the notes/essays/handouts you have on your visual/oral text that are connected to character. You may need to rewrite or reorder this material as you go.

Visual/Oral Text Essay – Character (20 minutes)
Now you are familiar with your notes write a plan of how you might answer one of the following questions:

1. *Analyse how a character or individual is influenced to make decisions in a text (or texts) you have studied.*

   OR

2. *Analyse how the growth of a relationship affects the climax in a text (or texts) you have studied.*

SESSION 17

Visual/Oral Text Essay – Theme (1 hour)
Answer the following question using the plan you wrote in Session 15. Don't forget to quickly check over your plan in case you missed something.

1. *Analyse how a character or individual is influenced to make decisions in a text (or texts) you have studied.*

   OR

2. *Analyse how the growth of a relationship affects the climax in a text (or texts) you have studied.*

SESSION 18

Quick Fire – Visual/Oral text (1 hour)
Answer the following question as though you are in an examination. You have 1 hour to complete the essays – don't forget to plan!

Analyse how atmosphere is established and maintained in a text (or texts) you have studied.

SESSION 19

Improving your work (1 hour)
Look through your year's work and find an essay (from either class work/previous examinations/study) that you have not done well.

a Reread the essay.

b Reread the comments made by your teacher.

c Using a red pen, mark parts of the essay that you know are not done well.

d Using a different colour pen, mark the parts of the essay you know are done well.

e Spend 10 minutes going through your notes looking for information to improve this essay.

f Rewrite the essay.

ISBN 9780170244213

SESSION 20

Close Reading Recap (1 hour)
Complete Recap Activity 7 from your downloaded *Achievement English @ Year 12 Revision Pack.*

Complete Close Reading Activity 7 from your downloaded *Achievement English @ Year 12 Revision Pack.*

SESSION 21

Recap your Visual/Oral Text (1 hour)
Spend some time reading over the work you have done on your Visual/Oral Text. Read any class notes, handouts etc you may have. Read through essays you have written, paying particular attention to areas you could improve. Spend some time learning key quotes.

SESSION 22

Recap your Written Text (1 hour)
Spend some time reading over the work you have done on your Written Text. Read through the text you are using. Read any class notes, handouts etc you may have. Read through essays you have written, paying particular attention to areas you could improve. Spend some time learning key quotes.

SESSION 23

Close Reading Recap (1 hour)
Complete Recap Activity 8 from your downloaded *Achievement English @ Year 12 Revision Pack.*

Complete Close Reading Activity 8 from your downloaded *Achievement English @ Year 12 Revision Pack.*

SESSION 24

Recap your Visual/Oral Text (1 hour)
Spend some time reading over the work you have done on your Visual/Oral Text. Read any class notes, handouts etc you may have. Read through essays you have written, paying particular attention to areas you could improve. Spend some time learning key quotes.

SESSION 25

Quick Fire – Visual/Oral text (1 hour)
Answer one of the following questions as though you are in an examination. You have 1 hour to complete the essay – don't forget to plan!

1. *Analyse how the beginning AND ending of a text show an important change in a character or individual in a text (or texts) you have studied.*

   OR

2. *Analyse how important techniques are used to engage your emotions in a text (or texts) you have studied.*

SESSION 26

Improving your work (1 hour)
Look through your year's work and find an essay (from either class work/previous examinations/study) that you have not done well.

a Reread the essay.
b Reread the comments made by your teacher.
c Using a red pen, mark parts of the essay that you know are not done well.
d Using a different colour pen, mark the parts of the essay you know are done well.
e Spend 10 minutes going through your notes looking for information to improve this essay.
f Rewrite the essay.

SESSION 27

Close Reading Recap (1 hour)
Complete Recap Activity 9 from your downloaded *Achievement English @ Year 12 Revision Pack.*

Complete Close Reading Activity 9 from your downloaded *Achievement English @ Year 12 Revision Pack.*

SESSION 28

Spend some time looking back through this book for activities that you have not completed during the year.

If you have completed them all spend time learning the Language Lists on pages 158-163.

SESSION 29

The Weakest Link (1 hour)
Choose the text (written or visual) that you feel is your weakest – be honest!

Spend this session going back over the work you have on this text. Re-read notes and handouts to familiarise yourself with the content again.

Now look carefully at the essays you have written on this text. Evaluate each one and look for where it could be improved.

Learn some quotes/phrases from the text that might be useful in the examination.

SESSION 30

Your last hour! Yay! Choose something you want to spend an hour 'brushing up on'. It may be something you feel you need a bit of extra time on, something you like, something you missed …

We know that you are as well prepared as possible for your Year 11 external assessments.

GOOD LUCK! See you in Year 13…

ISBN 9780170244213